The Black Death

A Captivating Guide to the Deadliest Pandemic in Medieval Europe and Human History

© **Copyright 2019**

All Rights Reserved. No part of this book may be reproduced in any form without permission in writing from the author. Reviewers may quote brief passages in reviews.

Disclaimer: No part of this publication may be reproduced or transmitted in any form or by any means, mechanical or electronic, including photocopying or recording, or by any information storage and retrieval system, or transmitted by email without permission in writing from the publisher.

While all attempts have been made to verify the information provided in this publication, neither the author nor the publisher assumes any responsibility for errors, omissions or contrary interpretations of the subject matter herein.

This book is for entertainment purposes only. The views expressed are those of the author alone, and should not be taken as expert instruction or commands. The reader is responsible for his or her own actions.

Adherence to all applicable laws and regulations, including international, federal, state and local laws governing professional licensing, business practices, advertising and all other aspects of doing business in the US, Canada, UK or any other jurisdiction is the sole responsibility of the purchaser or reader.

Neither the author nor the publisher assumes any responsibility or liability whatsoever on the behalf of the purchaser or reader of these materials. Any perceived slight of any individual or organization is purely unintentional.

Free Bonus from Captivating History (Available for a Limited time)

Hi History Lovers!

Now you have a chance to join our exclusive history list so you can get your first history ebook for free as well as discounts and a potential to get more history books for free! Simply visit the link below to join.

Captivatinghistory.com/ebook

Also, make sure to follow us on Facebook, Twitter and Youtube by searching for Captivating History.

Contents

INTRODUCTION 1

CHAPTER 1 – THE FIRST PANDEMICS 4
    What Is a Pandemic? 5
    The Justinian Plague 5
    The Black Death 7
    The Third Pandemic 8
    Concerns of Today 9

CHAPTER 2 – THE BLACK DEATH 10
    Types 11
        Bubonic Plague *11*
        Septicemic Plague *11*
        Pneumonic Plague *11*
    Symptoms 12
    Means of Spreading Infection 13
    Still Around 14

CHAPTER 3 – THE UNLIKELY USE OF THE BLACK DEATH 17

A Different Kind of Source 18
Placing the Blame 18
The Siege of Caffa 19
Ramifications for the Horrific Use of the Black Death in War 21

CHAPTER 4 – RUMORS AND ARRIVAL 23

Death on the Primary Trade Routes 24
The Infamous Arrival – More Than a Ship 27
Failure to Contain the Problem 28
A Lack of Understanding and Preparation 30

CHAPTER 5 – PERCEPTIONS VS. THE REALITY 34

Religious Beliefs 35
The First Solutions 37
The Rise of Flagellation to Atone 37
Scapegoats of the Plague 38
Plague Doctors 41

CHAPTER 6 – THE ULTIMATE EQUALIZER 43

How the Wealthy and Powerful Sought to Escape the Inevitable ... 44
The Shame of Divine Rights 45
The Death of a Queen, Princess, and King 45
The Beauty and Brains of France 46
Two Birds with One Stone – The Difficulty of Filling the Role of Archbishop of Canterbury 47

CHAPTER 7 – STEALING THE FUTURE – PRINCESS JOAN 51

King Edward III and a World at War 52
Preparing for a Celebration 54
A Matter of Timing – Celebration Turns to Tragedy 56

CHAPTER 8 – DECLINE OF THE CATHOLIC CHURCH AND THE RISE OF MYSTICISM 61

Life Before the Black Death 62
Prestige Lost 64
The Rise of Uncertainty and Strange Beliefs 65

    The Church Loses Its Way 66

CHAPTER 9 – ART OF THE BLACK DEATH 68

    Petrarch's Profound Loss 68
    Boccaccio and *The Decameron* 70
    Fall of the New Siena Movement 72

CHAPTER 10 – THE FIRST QUARANTINE AND SUCCESSFUL CONTAINMENT 73

    Early Attempts 74
    Venice 74
    Landlocked Efforts 76
    Plague Cemeteries 77

CHAPTER 11 – BEYOND THE HUMAN TOLL 79

    Animals Affected by the Plague 79
        Losing Food and Protection with the Death of Domesticated Animals 80
        Wool Shortage 80
    Labor Shortage 81
    Wars Stopped 82
    A Stronger Future 83

CHAPTER 12 – LASTING EFFECTS ON EUROPE'S FUTURE 85

    Repopulation and the Roles of Women 86
    Biological Warfare 87
    The Name the Black Death 88
    The Black Death in Literature and Media 89
        Nursery Rhymes and Other Legacies of the Black Death 90
        The Masquerade of the Red Death 91

CONCLUSION 94

BIBLIOGRAPHY 99

Introduction

The Black Death was one of the first recorded pandemics in Europe after the fall of the Roman Empire. All across the continent, people learned just how gruesome and horrific disease could be as the plague crossed the boundaries of countries and the lines established by society, killing everyone equally. It showed that no one—not even archbishops and kings—were immune from its grasp. The ferocity with which the plague swept across the continent, even reaching the shores of England, demonstrated how unprepared they were for something on such a large scale. It was the first time that a major disease would strike the majority of the continent after the fall of the Roman Empire, but it would not be the last.

Today, it is easy to look back on the superstition and fear that drove the people to believe some of the strangest things and to act in ways that are completely unacceptable now and lead us to wonder how anyone could have been so irrational.

In the beginning, people believed the plague was an isolated incident and that following through on a few religious traditions would protect them. The ailment first struck sailors and other people not known for being the most moral or religious people. Then the illness began to spread from port cities to surrounding areas. Entire villages were wiped out, and the terrifying plague did not seem to regard class, status, or religion. People began to panic as even monarchs and religious leaders died from a disease that spread faster than it could be detected.

Of course, we have a much better understanding of what caused the Black Death today. The fleas were the primary problem, although there is some debate over what animal was the primary carriers of fleas. Some say it was the mouse; others say rats. The truth is that any animal that could carry fleas would have been a threat, including people.

The effects of the plague are still felt today. With many historians estimating that about a third of the population of Europe was killed during the first pandemic, the event shaped the world that it touched. Nor was it a problem only in Europe, as word of the disease preceded its arrival. The people who heard the rumors of the death in foreign cities believed that it was a plague for the heathens. As it began to kill hundreds, then thousands, then entire towns, there appeared to be no clear reason for the cause. People panicked, looking for any scapegoat to blame as the population dwindled on an entire continent.

While the Black Death inspired some of the worst acts of humanity, it also was the beginning of some preventative practices that we still use today. As word of the plague spread, one particularly intelligent traveler realized that part of the problem was the introduction of people with the illness into healthy towns. Understanding that there was a correlation, he began the first quarantine to keep a town safe. It was also noticed that those who had survived the deadly plague were not susceptible to it later. While it would take centuries to understand how to use this information, exposure to a particularly nasty ailment is exactly what vaccines today provide those who get them.

Over the next few centuries, the bubonic plague would return several times. Although it was incredibly deadly, it never again had the same catastrophic effect on the European population. People began to study it from a scientific perspective instead of the same superstitious angle or religious fatalism, making it possible to understand exactly what was causing the deaths. Today, those in the medical profession can easily treat the bubonic plague if they realize what it is early enough. With examples of the illness occurring in many nations during the last decade, including the US, the Black Death is not gone, but it is no longer the death sentence that it once was.

Chapter 1 – The First Pandemics

It is nearly certain that there were ailments in Europe that caused mass deaths and panic prior to the arrival of the Black Death. However, there were not many recorded instances of a pandemic that was so devastating that it wiped out a large percentage of the population. One of the reasons why the plague was able to take so many lives was that people believed in religion and superstition instead of science. At the time, science was not nearly advanced enough to help prevent or cure disease, leaving people to feel powerless as loved ones died off and then fell ill themselves.

Many of the movies today about outbreaks and sudden plagues killing off large portions of the population are based in large part on the Black Death. While it definitely did not spread at the rate portrayed in movies and shows, it did seem like it would eventually wipe out all life—not just humans. History teaches us that it is possible for plagues to quickly wipe out life, but we have also come a long way since the last pandemic, hopefully making it unlikely that history will be repeated.

What Is a Pandemic?

According to the World Health Organization, "A pandemic is the worldwide spread of a new disease." Influenza, commonly called the flu, is one such example. Sometimes the flu can be particularly potent, but it is an illness that people have come to anticipate and strive to prevent. This kind of influenza is more potent than seasonal influenza, but we are typically warned about it once medical professionals realize there is a particularly virulent strain moving around the globe, affecting people of all ages, not just the elderly and young children.

However, the worst examples of pandemics were far more lethal and helped to shape the world we live in today. Nearly everyone in the Western world has heard of the Black Death, even if they don't know exactly when it struck. It wiped out a third of the population in Europe and affected the Europeans for more than a century. However, it was a pandemic, and it did not just affect Europe. The bubonic plague struck three different times in history, leaving deep scars everywhere that it thrived. It has touched nearly every continent and still exists today, but we are fortunate enough to have a much better understanding of medicine and illness and can treat the disease successfully if it is caught early.

The Justinian Plague

It is perhaps not nearly as well-known as the Black Death, but the first recorded pandemic to touch Europe occurred between 541 and 544 CE in the Byzantine Empire. The people considered themselves Romans since they were the continuation of the eastern half of the Roman Empire, which survived nearly a millennium longer than the Western Roman Empire. They were just as intelligent and gifted as the Romans that we know about today, and they were capable of a lot more in the way of innovations and intellectual pursuits than the parts of Europe during the Middle Ages. As the rest of Europe had descended into superstition and the Dark Ages, the Byzantine Empire continued the architectural, intellectual, and scientific endeavors of the Romans. Despite believing in science, the people living in Constantinople did not know about microscopic organisms and were at a complete loss when people began dying from a mysterious ailment in 541 AD.

Called the Justinian Plague after the ruler of the time, Justinian I, the plague worked its way through the population at an alarming rate. It is believed that this particular plague originated in Central Asia before spreading to Ethiopia, a lively trade center, via sea routes. From Ethiopia, the plague followed trade routes to Egypt, a province of the Byzantine Empire and a major hub for trade with the rest of Europe. From Egypt, the plague spread along trade routes, both in the Mediterranean and then along northern Africa into the Byzantine Empire.

It was the first time that the bubonic plague struck the continent, but it was much worse near Constantinople, which today is called Istanbul. The trade centers in much of Europe were much smaller, so the effect on most of the continent was not as dire. As it affected the Byzantine Empire which spread from eastern Europe across the Middle East and into northern Africa, it did not leave the kind of impression that the next visitation would mark in European history. It is attributed with helping lead to the decline of the empire though. Famine and social issues became another concern, which would be mimicked in the next major iteration, with much greater devastating and memorable losses to Europeans.

Minor outbreaks would occasionally arise over roughly the next 200 years, but they were largely so minor that they are little more than a footnote in history. The lives lost were no less important, but the scale was too small to be noted. However, this would change in the 14th century.

The Black Death

The Justinian Plague was devasting to the people who were affected, but it was largely unnoticed by most of Europe. Over the next 800 years, things would change significantly in Europe, with people gravitating toward cities. Christianity began to splinter, with Rome rising as the new hub for European Christianity: Catholicism. This would play a very important role in how people would come to understand the plague.

Rumors of an eastern plague had reached Europe, particularly the Italian ports, but it seemed like a distant problem until it arrived on their shores. The clergy had some knowledge of the plague that devasted the Byzantine Empire during the 6th century, but most of the population was unaware of what had occurred so long ago in a place so far away. The sudden arrival of a plague that moved impossibly fast caused a panic. Most of the people would not have known the term pandemic, but that was exactly what was occurring. Notable people in Europe, both on the continent and on the isles, died with very little warning that anything was wrong. Once a person started to show signs of the illness, it was too late to save them.

The death toll was unimaginable, and people found they did not have the right tools to cope with what was happening. The Black Death lasted from 1346 to 1353, then seemed to largely disappear, only to flare up occasionally around the continent.

It was the first time that a plague was documented to the extent that we now see today. One of the most renowned writers of the time, Giovanni Boccaccio, wrote about the plague in one of his most famous works, *The Decameron*. It provides a look into the mentality and terror that the disease wrought on a people who were not equipped to deal with any major disaster and certainly not something that required science to cure.

At the time, it came to be called the pestilence, but it would leave an indelible mark on all of Europe. As people looked back at the history books, they would eventually declare the disease to be the Black Death. Today, it is nearly impossible to imagine just how horrific the bubonic plague was because we have never experienced anything comparable. Even the AIDS scare in the 1980s and 1990s was not nearly as devastating as the Black Death. Yet that does not keep people from fearing that it will happen again. The span of centuries has done nothing to lessen the fear and horror that the first Black Death inspired on several continents.

The Third Pandemic

Though the bubonic plague would occasionally return, the next time it reached the level of a pandemic was in China in the middle of the 19th century. The familiar disease was still not entirely understood more than 500 years later. This time, it would ravage the countries in Asia and Australia. It began in a remote area of China, but it began to spread along trade routes for opium and tin. Like tentacles stretching out from the source, it went in several different directions, reaching Hong Kong in 1894 and Bombay in 1896.

Just like the last pandemic, the bubonic plague spread to port cities around the world, but it did not have the same effect in places that it had previously ravaged. It caused grave concerns in Australia and much of Asia, but it was the poorer countries that really suffered because they did not have the means to fight the plague. The place hardest hit was India. An estimated 15 million people died during this third pandemic that ended around 1959. Unlike the previous pandemics, the plague seemed to disappear, then rear its head again when people thought it was safe. This made the disease difficult to fight and is the reason why so many lives were lost.

Concerns of Today

Science has made it far easier to fight disease, but it also has made it significantly easier to spread. Besides biological weapons, modern innovations like airplanes and large-scale globalization have made it so that disease can easily move to a new location before anyone even knows that there is a problem. Movies and shows may contain an exaggeration of the pace with which illness usually spreads, but it does highlight just how susceptible we are if we aren't careful. This should serve more as a caution and a reminder to be careful and to monitor destinations before you visit them and after you return. Preventive actions like shots and monitoring your health can help one more quickly identify problems if something does emerge.

Chapter 2 – The Black Death

The bubonic plague has occasionally reappeared throughout history to remind humanity that nothing should be taken for granted. It left its mark on Europe, Asia, and Africa, with death tolls that are nearly unimaginable today. When we think about the Black Death, we think of it as a problem that has recurred in our history and not a concern for our future. We think of the people who suffered through the pain and panic as being unfortunate and ignorant because science had not progressed far enough to explain just what caused the plague. The events were more like a perfect storm that took the lives of many millions of people. However, as the previous chapter showed, the illness is not quite as remote in history as we would like to believe.

Understanding the bubonic plague is much easier today because technology has advanced well beyond the pseudo-science and mysticism of medieval Europe. Though there is some debate about various aspects of the disease, the annual diagnosis of people suffering from the disease does not leave much room for uncertainty about how the plague works.

Types

There are three types of plague, all of which are caused by Yersinia pestis, a bacterium. If untreated, all three of the types are usually deadly, even the least potent type, the bubonic plague, as history has amply demonstrated. This is in part because it does spread if untreated and can cause one of the more lethal forms.

Bubonic Plague

The most infamous form of the plague is the bubonic plague, and it is still the most common form. In this form, the bacterium attacks the lymph nodes. This plague derives its name from the swollen and painful lymph nodes that are infected, often called buboes. Patients with this type of plague will have swollen lymph nodes in their neck, under their arms, and around their groin. If it goes untreated, it can begin to infect other organs and vital systems, most notably the circulatory and respiratory systems.

Septicemic Plague

Considerably more dangerous than the bubonic plague, the bacterium infects and travels through the blood. This means that it spreads far more rapidly if it is not treated.

Pneumonic Plague

As the name suggests, this version of the illness starts by attacking the lungs. Of the three types, it is the least common and is always fatal if untreated. Its symptoms are similar to those of many other respiratory ailments, so it is another reason why you need to visit a doctor when you are having respiratory troubles.

Unlike the other two types, pneumonic plague is airborne, so you can catch it from being exposed to someone who has it and has been coughing near you. If it is determined that you have the pneumonic plague, you should let everyone who has been exposed to you recently know so they can be checked. It is easily the most dangerous form of the plague as it does not need another agent to transmit the disease between two people.

Symptoms

Each of the three types of plague has its own symptoms, which makes it easier to determine what type of the plague a person has. Incubation for the plague is between a day and a week. Typically, a person who contracts the ailment will start to show signs in less than a week, although for those with pneumatic plague, symptoms may present themselves within less than a day.

Nearly all sufferers begin by feeling cold or chills and have a fever early after the incubation period of the disease. They tend to be achy and get frequent or constant headaches during the early stages as well.

The bubonic plague got its name from the most obvious symptom that a sufferer exhibits—the swollen lymph nodes. In addition to swelling, the buboes will become tender and painful (even without additional pressure). When untreated, open sores can form that ooze pus.

Septicemic plague will start to show itself in much more alarming ways. For example, the sufferer will have visible bleeding under the skin or orifices, such as their nose, mouth, or anus. Their extremities tend to turn black (blackened fingers, toes, and nose are common signs that the ailment is progressing). It is often accompanied by apparent stomach ailments, such as vomiting and diarrhea.

One of the reasons that people tend to wait seeking help for pneumonic plague is that the initial symptoms present themselves as being no different from so many other respiratory illnesses. The sufferer will begin to cough and have trouble breathing. At some point, the coughs will include blood, which is an obvious sign that the illness is very serious and should not be ignored. Like those with septicemic plague, people who have pneumonic plague may also experience abdominal problems, including vomiting.

It is important to note that if the bubonic plague is left untreated, it is very likely to result in one or both of the other types. The bacterium will infect all parts of the body, as seen by the records from the Black Death. The earliest victims of the disease tended to have the bubonic plague, as their symptoms were swollen lymph nodes. However, it is also called the Black Death because so many of the victims clearly had the symptoms of septicemic plague after a few days. Their bodies began to be bloody and turn black even before they were dead. Over time, it is just as likely that the illness would have spread without fleas because so many people had bacteria in all of their vital systems, including the respiratory system. Based on the quickness with which the disease spread over time, and the fact that many of the victims were said to have shown signs within a day of coming into contact with someone who had the illness, it is very likely that pneumonic plague played as large a role as bubonic plague in wiping out a large percentage of the European population.

Means of Spreading Infection

Most people today know that the plague is carried by rats and mice and is transferred by fleas. This is true, but they are not the only vessels. Any animal that might attract fleas, particularly dogs and cats, are potential carriers. However, pneumonic plague is not transmitted through flea bites but through airborne pathogens. If exposed to someone with this form of the plague, you can contract it without any interaction of fleas.

It is believed that there was a combination of all three forms of the plague that wiped out much of Europe. It is very possible that some of the population could have contracted pneumonic plague and it spread to the lymph nodes, resulting in it looking like the bubonic plague. Those who contracted it through the air likely would have died much quicker as their lungs would have begun to fail in the early stages of the illness. With an incubation period that can be less than 24 hours, people can begin to show signs of having contracted the disease within a single day. This is why it is so critical to get diagnosed as early as possible after the onset of symptoms and to let others know if they have been potentially exposed.

Still Around

One of the most haunting things about the Black Death is that it has never disappeared. People today tend to think of it as a horrific event that occurred in the long distant past. Even those who are acutely aware of the toll it took during the 19th century and into the 20th century think of it as a problem that science has conquered.

This is not at all true though.

The bubonic plague has never been designated as a disease that has been eradicated. With vaccinations having rendered smallpox, polio, and a few other more "modern" diseases a thing of the past, many people assume that an infection that caused such an unfathomable death toll centuries ago remained in the past. But the bubonic plague is still an ailment that people today suffer from—on the majority of inhabited continents—and people should be aware that the plague is very much an illness that can be contracted today.

Because it is a bacterial disease, there is no vaccination for the bubonic plague. In developed nations, it is not likely to be fatal if it is caught early enough. Since it is a bacterial infection, medical professionals can treat the bubonic plague with antibiotics, and patients have a very high rate of survival today. If it is not caught early though, it can result in serious health hazards, loss of limbs, and death.

Here are a few statistics about the plague based on several different health organizations.

> - The World Health Organization continues to track the plague and has released the following statistics, which are updated regularly:

o Between 2010 and 2015, there were a reported 3,248 cases. Of those, 584 people died. While the number of reported cases is an incredibly small percentage of the world's population, the fatality rate for those cases was nearly 18%. Most of the areas with fatalities were in developing countries or areas with little to no medical options.

o The bubonic plague has a fatality rate of between 30–60% when untreated. There are always long-lasting effects for those who survive without treatment, including a lower quality of life. Pneumonic plague is almost 100% fatal if untreated.

o The majority of the reported cases of plague are in Peru, Madagascar, and the Democratic Republic of the Congo.

- There have been reported cases of the plague in many countries that are considered modern (and probably thought to be safe), including China, India, Mongolia, Vietnam, and the US. The last epidemic of the plague occurred in 2006 in the Democratic Republic of the Congo, resulting in an estimated 50 deaths.

- According to the US Center for Disease Control, the US has an average of 1 to 17 cases every year, with more than 80% of the reported cases being bubonic plague. There is no set age limit for who can contract it, but 50% of the reported cases are in people between 12 and 45 years old.

- Though it is closely linked in people's minds today with Europe, there actually has not been a reported case of the disease in Europe in recent years.

Remember, the plague can be transferred through parasitic insects, but that is not—and has never been—the sole means of contracting the disease. The most fatal version is contracted without requiring any exposure to fleas and acts much faster. Being aware that it has other means of spreading can one help detect the problem earlier so that proper treatment can be sought. Just because it is treatable does not mean that it isn't dangerous or even fatal.

Chapter 3 – The Unlikely Use of the Black Death

One of the most interesting, and certainly most unexpected, stories out of the horror of the Black Death is not about the aftereffects (though they are fascinating and are still visible today) or the way it acted as a great equalizer. Today, we often consider biological warfare to be a modern development, something that no one could do before technology evolved enough to weaponize the use of diseases against the enemy. However, one of the ways not often discussed for its introduction into Europe is the possibility that the Black Death was weaponized and targeted a certain group of people. This biological warfare was crude, and clearly, the people who used it did not have the same reservations about killing anyone who came into contact with it that someone from the military might have had. Yet it was recorded as a weapon used during the siege of a city, and the ramifications certainly went beyond what was originally intended. This serves not only as a lesson about history but about the continued used of biological weapons and how irresponsible it is to attempt to use them because the consequences can go beyond those that are intended.

A Different Kind of Source

What is known about one of the ways the Black Death reached Europe comes from the memoirs of an Italian merchant named Gabriele de' Mussi. As the plague spread in areas outside of Europe and eventually made its way to the continent, de' Mussi never left Piacenza, Italy. This means that his accounts with the descriptions of events and the disease were not influenced by travels abroad. The significance of this is that the Black Death very likely arrived on the continent in more ways than through the ailing sailors arriving in the port city of Messina, Sicily. Given how the plague had spread to many different areas outside of Europe, it is almost guaranteed that it entered through multiple locations too. But people prefer to have a single definitive source, and that has led to speculation about a single point of entry for the deadly disease. We will explore a couple, though this scenario is the one that became the most well known and most well documented after the plague began to spread. Still, given how quickly the disease spread across the continent, it is it far more likely that there was more than one instance of the plague entering the population of Europe.

Given that there are at least two different methods through which the disease reached the continent, it shows just how devastating the effects were as it spread rapidly from two different areas, instead of just having a single source.

Placing the Blame

As will be covered later, many people believed that the plague was a punishment from God or a plot by a small minority of people. Well ahead of the arrival of the fatal illness in Europe, it was creating problems and decimating populations around the known world. During the 1340s, the population of Crimea was under the threat of the Black Death, which had created a panic.

In Crimea, an estimated 85,000 people had died because of the illness. There are no records of why the blame was placed on a few European merchants, but it is known that the Tartars (the predominant population of Crimea) decided that they needed to confront Christian merchants working in the city called Tana. It is possible that the hatred was based in the very hostile relationship between the Tartars and the Genoese, and the ensuing confrontation may have been entirely unrelated to the Black Death in the beginning.

The merchants working in a portion of the market made up primarily of Genoese merchants fled when faced by the Tartars. They had a safe haven in the coastal city of Caffa (currently Feodosia). With a large economic interest in the area, the Genoese had created a fortified location where they could have a foothold in Crimea and safety if the need arose.

The Siege of Caffa

De' Mussi provides an account of the siege that is both horrifying and intriguing. While much of his memoir is more of a moral dictum and calls for people to repent their sins, it shows that there was an understanding by the more educated people that the plague was also, at least in part, a result of human cruelty.

As the Tartars began their siege of Caffa, the plague followed them. Outside of Caffa, they began to die in large numbers. According to de' Mussi, this caused the Tartars to rethink their strategy and to reprioritize.

> The dying Tartars, Stunned and stupefied by the immensity of the disaster brought about by the disease, and realizing that they had no hope of escape, lost interest in the siege. But they ordered corpses to be placed in catapults and lobbed into the city in the hope that the intolerable stench would kill everyone inside. What seemed like mountains of dead were thrown into the city, and the Christians could not hide or flee

or escape from them, although they dumped as many of the bodies as they could in the sea...one infected man could carry the poison to others, and infect people and places with the disease by look alone.

...As it happened, among those who escaped from Caffa by boat were a few sailors who had been infected with the poisonous disease. Some boats were bound for Genoa, others went to Venice and to other Christian areas. When the sailors reached these places and mixed with the people there, it was as if they had brought evil spirits with them...Thus death entered through the windows, and as cities and towns were depopulated their inhabitants mourned their dead neighbours.

According to de' Mussi's memoir, the siege was not sustainable because so many of those waiting at the gates were dying from the disease. Since they could not attack the Christians, the Tartars decided to head home but not before finding a far more horrific way of making the Christians pay for their hubris. With too many bodies to take home, the Tartars used their catapults to launch their dead into the stronghold of Caffa. The translation does make it sound as if de' Mussi believed that the Tartars just wanted the Christians to deal with the same horrific sights and smells. It is very likely though that the Tartars knew exactly what they were doing: the corpses were being used as a part of biological warfare. They knew that the people in the city would have much worse to contend with than decaying corpses and an unpleasant smell. They intentionally infected the people in the city since the fortifications kept the Christians from being exposed to the same horrors of the Black Death that they were dealing with. At this time, the disease had not reached the shores of Europe, so the Europeans did not know just how horrific the disease really was.

That would all change once the few survivors who fled Caffa reached Europe. The Black Death was not divine retribution as most of Europe would think. It is almost certain that the introduction of the disease, at least in part, was the result of early successful and intentional biological warfare. Some even speculate that the sailors that arrived in Sicily were some of those who fled from the attack, failing to escape in time and bringing the disease with them.

Ramifications for the Horrific Use of the Black Death in War

De' Mussi's memoirs provide some very unexpected and educational information as they show that there was an awareness that it was not just a punishment from the Christian God. He believed that the plague that wiped out so much of Europe was a direct result of the siege on the single Genoese stronghold at Caffa. There was another explanation that was largely ignored, and it involved what most Europeans called heathens, whether they were Muslim, Buddhist, or any other religion that was not Christian. If the Black Death was a punishment, it came from another group of people, not from the Christian God, as many of the less educated people believed. The people who were in charge were unwilling to condemn the heathens outside of Europe since it was economically not ideal to do cut off trade with them. To keep lining their pockets, the powerful and wealthy ignored this aspect of the introduction of the Black Death so that they could continue to benefit financially. Those who knew better preferred to blame sin and transgressions instead of cutting off trade with a country that helped kill between a quarter and a half of Europe's population.

In part, they viewed it as evidence that the heathens were horrible. This did not dissuade European merchants from maintaining relations and trading with them abroad, but it was used against those heathens who chose to live in Europe among the Christians.

It is certain that some of the first instances of the Black Death in Europe began following the Siege of Caffa. The next chapter covers the more widely accepted series of events, but it is almost certain that the events in Caffa played as much of a role in the introduction and spread of the Black Death in Europe as the ship that docked in Messina on that fateful day of October 1347.

Chapter 4 – Rumors and Arrival

The Black Death refers to the different types of plague during a single point in European history. The plague first spread between 1346 and 1353, with a few years between outbreaks. It would continue to crop up and take lives periodically, but these were the most devasting periods where a significant portion of the population perished. If a person fell ill with the disease, it was almost as good as a death sentence. People today call it the bubonic plague, but it is really more accurate to call it the plague because all three types were certainly present. The people who died the quickest quite likely contracted the pneumonic plague, but the signs for the bubonic plague were often present as the bacterium did not attack just a single aspect of the body. There were a few people who survived, but they were in a very small minority. Although the name was not used during the time when the illness was rampant in Europe, the term refers almost exclusively to the 14th century when the disease took the lives of up to half of the entire European population.

This is perhaps ironic as the Europeans had years of warning leading up to its arrival. However, the problem was only known by a very small percentage of the population, and even to them, the disease was killing people in a foreign place. To them, it was an unfortunate instance of problems that only the heathens of the East had to contend with, and some believed that the reason for the affliction was because the heathens did not have the same religious beliefs. Their gods were not as powerful as the one worshipped in Europe, so the people in the East were left to suffer. Soon, the Europeans would learn just how wrong their indifference, detached ideas, and feelings of religious superiority were.

Death on the Primary Trade Routes

Long before the plague reached the continent, the educated and elite class of Europe had been hearing about it. The rare merchant who was brave enough to journey out into the world returned to Europe with horrific stories of a disease that would not create the kind of alarm that it should have. The stories were too far removed and the danger intangible. Time would soon prove that the rumors from the trade routes should have been heeded instead of being dismissed. There were some merchants who were able to provide some details of just how rapidly the plague had progressed, as well as being able to list some of the signs of the disease. It is very likely that merchants did relay certain details, but their audience only heard it as a misfortune befalling heathens living in foreign places. There was some sympathy for the people, but it meant nothing to the people of Europe.

Tales undoubtedly included information on just how quickly death came to those who were marked by the large buboes and that a week later nearly everyone who was marked would die. With such a high mortality rate among the afflicted in far-off places, there was plenty of reason for the peoples of Europe to feel sympathy. The problem was that this also should have served as a warning. Not everyone who suffered died. The fact that merchants who had traveled to the areas that were being affected and lived to provide descriptions should have been a warning that it was possible for the disease to travel.

On some level, there were people who were aware that the "Great Pestilence" that was plaguing other countries along the trade routes could be a problem. The ports had some level of cautionary measures as they were on the lookout for signs that sailors and those arriving on vessels in the port were infected. After all, sailors had also come ashore with word about the mysterious pestilence affecting foreign cities, so the news came from several sources and not just from the merchants who survived the trade routes.

The problem was that there was a certain level of blissful ignorance and false sense of protection, as the disease had been plaguing other nations along the major trade routes. Countries that had been great trade partners, such as China, India, Persia, Syria, and Egypt had all experienced the worst of the disease. At the same time though, all of them were governed by heathens, and their gods were not the God of Europe. On some level, Europeans believed that they would be spared because they thought their God was protecting them from the evils being spread elsewhere. The fact that they remained the one plague-free large partner along the trade routes was proof that their religion was the right one.

What they failed to notice was that the plague was making its way from its point of origin in China and spreading west. India and Persia were still some distance away, so that did not make the Europeans wary. By the time it had reached Egypt, however, they should have been far more cautious because the trip across the Mediterranean Sea was not nearly so distant as the land route to China. Sailors making the crossing would certainly not all perish before they arrived on the shores of Europe.

As the plague progressed, the elite of Europe who had heard of it felt a false sense of security. Even if it did reach their shores, they believed that they would still be safe. This sense of invulnerability belied a larger problem. With few people being educated in Europe, there were too few people who took any kinds of precautions. The lack of preparation would be part of the reason why the disease would have such an unprecedented impact on so many European nations. The vast majority of people who did not live near ports were entirely unaware of the disease, making them incredibly susceptible to exposure once it began to move inland.

This sense of religious superiority would also end up turning against the people of Europe. The vast majority of the people would see the Black Death as a sign of God's wrath. The elite would be at a loss for how to escape it because it quickly proved that even their more remote castles, monasteries, and lands were not immune from the plague. It was also one of the major turning points in the political power structure. As people watched their loved ones die a gruesome death and then suffered through it themselves, they lost faith in the teachings by the elite.

No one could predict exactly what would happen once the disease finally reached European shores, and their lack of foresight was what would eventually cause so many deaths. It was nearly a certainty that the plague would reach the European ports. The merchants and traders along the traditional paths either did not survive the trip or would not attempt to travel when they were ill, which meant that the plague likely did not enter Europe by land. The greatest risk of the disease reaching the shores was through those who traded along the Mediterranean Sea. It is almost certain that the Genoese traders who survived Caffa helped introduce the plague to some parts of Europe, but it is known for certain that one of the first recorded instances occurred in a port in Sicily called Messina. Given how quickly the disease spread, it is probable that there were multiple ships that brought the plague to the shore, but this particular port was the one that went down in infamy as the bringer of the deadliest disease to ever strike Europe.

The Infamous Arrival – More Than a Ship

Until October 1347, the "Great Pestilence" was nothing more than a misfortune that struck other nations on other continents. It had been working its way west but had arrived in northern Africa first, completely missing Europe. That did not mean that people along the coastal cities had not been guarded against it. Even those people who were not as well educated had heard whispered rumors of a terrible disease because sailors would have heard about the epidemic when they were away from home. Having heard of the plague, they knew that they were at risk, but they did not take any precautions with the ships as they arrived and departed.

During that October, a dozen ships arrived and docked in Messina. These twelve ships would later be dubbed "the death ships," and there were many witnesses to the horrors that they brought into the port. The vast majority of the sailors on the ships were already dead when the ships arrived, their corpses showing horrific evidence of how painful their deaths would have been. Worse still were the sailors who were still alive. Not much better off than the corpses, they were clearly suffering from what their mates had already endured. The poor sailors were clearly unwell as they were covered in buboes. The welts were large, black, and oozed both pus and blood. The witnesses to the condition of these sailors were mortified because the disease that had been whispered about on foreign shores had finally reached their own coast.

As soon as the authorities at the port realized what was aboard the ships, they demanded the immediate removal of the ships, no matter what state the sailors were in. No attempt was made to treat the sailors or to let them remain in the port, as the disease could potentially infect others. By driving the ships from their shores without giving the dying sailors a new destination, the authorities were ensuring that other locations would suffer the same fate.

However, the ships had already been docked, and people had been aboard them to witness the appalling conditions on the ships. For a long time, historians speculated that fleas on the ships were the source of the plague that made its way to the shores of Sicily that day. We now know what scientists have since learned as they studied the pandemic and that is that the plague could also be contracted through the air. No rats, mice, or other rodents would need to have made their way to the shore, which would have been difficult considering how quickly the ships were removed. It is very likely that many of the first cases were actually a result of pneumonic plague for those people who saw the dying sailors, particularly if they were in the final throes of death. The bodies of the living would have been releasing numerous fluids into the air through their pus- and blood-filled wounds, incessant coughing, and vomit and diarrhea. Each of the ships would have had more than enough airborne pathogens to have infected the people who witnessed the grim sights aboard them.

Failure to Contain the Problem

One of the earliest problems was that no one tried to contain the plague in the early days. Afraid to remain where they were and potentially be exposed, people fled to other cities. Merchants and tradesmen, however, continued with their daily routines. By the time Shakespeare wrote *Romeo and Juliet*, the continent was wise to the need for quarantines, and the result in that story was that the priest was held up due to a quarantine so that Juliet did not get word that Romeo was still alive. There was no such safety protocol in place when the Black Death first struck Europe.

Many of the people in Europe who knew about the problems abroad did not think that it was ever going to be a problem that would affect them. This lack of forethought and planning meant that they did not bother to study the ways that the disease could be brought under control. While the Black Death killed large portions of the population around the world during this pandemic, few were as tragically affected as Europe. Some of the other countries and civilizations had learned from the earlier Justinian Plague, but the people of Europe had largely ignored what wasn't on their doorstep. This meant they were woefully unprepared to contend with a rapidly spreading disease. The plague killed large portions of all the populations where it spread, but no places recorded the number of deaths seen in Europe and China. As the location where the plague originated, China had no time to prepare. Europe, on the other hand, should have seen the disease traveling toward their shores. They chose to believe that their God would protect them rather than prepare for the possibility of the disease reaching their home.

Many today think that it could have been as easily controlled as eradicating fleas and other parasitic insects, but of course, they did not have the same understanding that we do. It was the Dark Ages of Europe, and science had been largely ignored since the fall of Rome. Superstition and religion ruled their lives, and the vast majority of the population were illiterate. Still, the fact that people today think that the death toll could have been significantly reduced by better pest control shows that people still don't take the time to fully understand the risks of pandemics. There is no doubt that fleas and other carriers spread the disease, but that was not the sole means of the pestilence spreading. The plague is also airborne, so those who tended to people whose lungs were affected were breathing in the plague—it wasn't just the fleas that were the problem. This kind of half-understanding is just as dangerous today as it was centuries ago.

Had the ship been allowed to stay in port and the bodies disposed of and a quarantine established, the plague would very likely have still reached Europe. It was all but an inevitability. Perhaps it might not have been so disastrous if the ships had remained at port. With twelve ships carrying dead sailors and with no port that would welcome them, it meant that the ships would end up in other areas along the shore. Even if all of the sailors were dead, the ships would still have reached other locations along the coast. And once there, people would board the ships to find the grisly sight, and the disease would reach other victims. The damage could have been minimized by keeping the ships in Messina, but there was not enough understanding of the illness, let alone the ability to keep it contained. The sending of the ships back into the Mediterranean Sea would prove to be a devastating decision for the entire continent.

One of the main lessons that can be taken from this today is that problems cannot be simply sent away. It is very likely that this was not the only incident, and all of the blame for what was to come cannot be placed on the people of Messina. Often this is pointed to as the point where the Black Death finally reached the continent, but it is almost impossible that it was the only instance. There is even doubt that it was the first encounter. However, it is the point that has been passed down through history as the start of one of the most horrific events of European history.

A Lack of Understanding and Preparation

Despite having heard about the "Great Pestilence," no preparations were made to fight it should it ever reach European shores. There was adequate time had those who had heard of it tried to prepare for the disease, as many countries do today. The main problem was that Europe had not seen a major pandemic in hundreds of years. The Justinian Plague did not affect Europe much, and despite having occurred hundreds of years earlier, the people of Europe may have seen this as evidence that they were immune. Christianity had already started to splinter, and people considered the Christians of the Byzantine Empire to be heathens. The people of Europe and the people of the empire fought together against Muslims during the first few crusades. However, by the Fourth Crusade from 1202 to 1204, the European Christians decided to attack the empire. Around this time, the empire was experiencing the end of its time, though it was no longer nearly as powerful or large as it had been. Europe had proved they were more powerful than their neighbors, at least in their own minds.

This mentality was probably a large part of why the peoples of Europe felt it unnecessary to worry about the plague spreading throughout the rest of the world. There was certainly a hubris on the continent.

Other places suffered terribly from the disease, but none of them would suffer on the same scale as Europe. Those along the trade route likely took some precautions, though it is not well documented how they managed it. Many places had either suffered serious diseases or had heard of places that were devastated by disease. They had more experience, or at least more recent experience. When word returned to these places that there was a terrible disease that was taking a large toll, they would have done what they could to prepare instead of relying on luck, superstition, or divine intervention to keep them safe.

The lack of any recent far-reaching illness worked against the people of Europe. For centuries they had been rebuilding the lands after the fall of the Roman Empire. Repopulation was slow, but they were clearly progressing. Towns grew much slower in Europe than in other locations around the known world (Asia and Africa). In the 13th century, the number of towns in Europe was few, and the continent was still almost exclusively comprised of agrarian societies. The towns that dotted the European landscape were almost all fewer than 10,000 people.

Italy was among the first to reject the feudal lifestyle that was common in Europe leading up to the 13th century. That is where towns and cities began to grow as people began to seek their own fortune. It was easier to find work and to make a living when there were more people around. Ports drew the greatest number of people because trade was more profitable and there were far more options. The people in Europe were not as well educated in what the Romans had known about the risks of trading with foreign lands, so they did not have any real protection. As the towns and cities began to thrive, they were far more susceptible to the horrors of the plague than other places that had been affected. People lived in much closer quarters for protection against outsiders. The streets were narrow and the homes small, providing minimal protection. Perhaps one of the worst elements that set up the people of Europe for the spread of disease was the lack of protection for their primary sources of water, both for drinking and cleaning. Although bathing was not as common then, fresh water was required for drinking and cooking.

All of these elements would work against the people as the Black Death spread rapidly among them. They had found a way to protect themselves from invasions and humans, but they had not learned how to fight the kind of illness that was more familiar on other continents. This extends to how they managed the dead as well. The people of Europe were not prepared to deal with the number of dead bodies left in the wake of the disease. Having never dealt with this kind of death on any kind of comparable scale, they did not have the right means to deal with the vast number of bodies.

Giovanni Boccaccio provided a very succinct and sad description of the events during this time as people began to realize that the problem was much worse than they could have imaged.

> Dead bodies filled every corner. Most of them were treated in the same manner by the survivors, who were more concerned to get rid of their rotting bodies than moved by charity toward the dead. With the aid of porters, if they could get them, they carried the bodies out of the houses and laid them at the door; where every morning quantities of the dead might be seen. They were laid on biers or, as these were often lacking, on tables.

> Such was the multitude of corpses brought to the churches every day and almost every hour that there was not enough consecrated ground to give them burial.... The cemeteries were full they were forced to dig huge trenches, where they buried bodies by hundreds. Here they stowed them away like bales in the hold of a ship and covered them with a little earth, until the whole trench was full.

The Decameron provides a stark look at the way the plague swept through Europe, the feeling of panic and fear, and the inability of the people to deal with the scale of death it brought to their homes. Traditions had to be foregone since those who were infected were almost always dead within a week's time.

The mass graves were themselves a significant contributor to the continuation of the disease. Scavengers, rodents, and other animals would have been attracted to the stench and would have carried fleas farther from the source. As the animals brought the plague to new areas, they would die, forcing the parasites to look for other hosts. In this way, the people who died continued the cycle. The living passed on the disease through airborne pathogens, and the dead helped to further the spread through the parasites and animals that encountered them.

Chapter 5 – Perceptions Vs. The Reality

As Europeans became intimately familiar with the costs of the Black Death, the people found themselves completely unable to cope. Entire towns died as the disease swept through Europe, with very few areas remaining unaffected. Both continental Europe and the countries on the isles off the coast were affected. Despite the rumors about the Great Pestilence, even those who were better educated (largely the monarchs, the clergy of the Catholic Church, and those in port towns) had an incredibly limited understanding of just how dire the situation was. They had not prepared, and they had no answers as they sought a way to remove themselves from coming in contact with the deadly illness.

The peasants and people who worked the lands had no formal education. All of their knowledge about the world beyond their daily lives came from the clergy of the Church. Trying to understand just what was happening was impossible. Worse yet, the words of the Church failed to halt the progress of the illness as the death toll rose. For many, it must have seemed like the end of the world was coming, and this is when the nearly iron tight grip that the Church had on the majority of the populace began to wane. Later on, this book will provide further details on the religious fallout when it became apparent to the general population that the clergy who instructed them were not more knowledgeable about how to contain the problem. In the early days of the plague, however, people turned to their religious leaders in the hopes of being saved.

[handwritten: Today people look to CDC & Gov]

Religious Beliefs

Following the fall of the Western Roman Empire and the transition of the Eastern Roman Empire into what we now call the Byzantine Empire, the majority of Europe descended into a state that was similar to the world prior to the Roman invasion. Perhaps the most notable difference was that many of the areas that had been under Roman control became Christian. Christianity had spread across most of Europe after the sacking of Rome. Over time, the Catholic Church became the dominant power across Europe, particularly as regions returned to their smaller clusters once the Romans were gone. Countries like England and France began to take control with new monarchies filling the power vacuum.

During all of the wars and the establishment of other powers, Christianity was one of the few things that many people had in common. This is why the Church had such immense power. It was vastly different than what most Europeans consider Christianity today (there were five seats for the Catholic Church, not just the one in the Vatican as it is now), and it included the regions under the extensive control of the Romans who founded Constantinople. This was the time when the Church really began to grow and the schisms would start to form. While the empire grew and established itself, the little principalities over much of continental Europe fought to control their areas. With the numerous power struggles across the continent and isles, the people turned to religion for instruction and stability.

During the centuries before 1340, most people lived their daily lives just striving to survive. The elements of their lives that dealt with socialization, law, and morality came largely from the Church. People learned that only the Church could instruct them in matters of the soul, and they came to rely on that instruction to understand right and wrong. Since only the clergy were certain to be educated (even a number of monarchs were either illiterate or had a very limited ability to read), it fell on the Church and its representatives to know how to behave. Even activities as simple as eating should be accompanied by prayer. If someone dined without thanking the benign and loving God of Christ, they could face the vengeful wrath of the God of the Old Testament. After all, Christ had believed in the Old Testament; the New Testament was written by the men who survived after his death.

There are many instances of the Church misusing and abusing its power during this time, just as any group in power tends to do. As one of the few unifying areas of the daily lives of all the people, they had considerably more influence than the rulers and landowners. The men of the Church (women of the Church had virtually no power in Europe) had a say not only in what was the right behavior in life, but they also had a place to judge people after death. For example, people could be denied burial on holy grounds, which could mean they would never find peace after death. As people were instructed to believe that their existence after life was more important, many of the members of the population strove to at least appear moral in the eyes of their neighbors and the clergy.

The extensive power of the Catholic Church lasted for centuries, working its way into the very fabric of daily life for the vast majority of those who lived in Europe. When the plague arrived on the continent, people initially turned to the Church for salvation. The disease that had been a problem for distant heathens had now reached their shores and was killing Europeans in numbers that were previously unimaginable.

Used Jews as a scapegoat

The First Solutions

Terrified and looking for any kind of solution, the people initially followed the dictates of their familiar religion. At first, the Church began to find explanations for the disease. The people themselves were blamed, and it was the vengeful God of the Old Testament who was punishing them for their shortcomings and inadequacies. The people were told that their sins had led to the disease and that it would not be cured until they sincerely repented.

Hypocritically, while blaming the people and their sins for the plague, a lot of blame also fell on the Jewish population in Europe. It was said that they were the source for the plague. While they were not the only group that was blamed, they were the ones who received the greatest blame for the pandemic (despite the efforts of the Tartars who can possibly be directly linked to the arrival of the plague on the continent). Those in power did not want to lose money by stopping trade with other countries, so instead of placing some of the blame where it was due, they chose to use scapegoats to purge other religions and people from their borders.

The Rise of Flagellation to Atone

To address their own sins, people initially tried to live their lives more in line with how their clergy told them. As it became obvious that simple atonement was not adequate, more extreme measures were taken to appease their God. During 1348, people began to whip themselves to prove that they were sincerely sorry for the sins they had committed. Certain men became the primary means of providing the whipping service. They traveled to different towns to whip people who wanted to repent in the hopes that it would be adequate to protect them and their families from the Black Death.

The process was called flagellation, and the men who provided the service were called Flagellants. Men who provided the service used a whip made of leather thongs, usually with more than one thong to each whip. The towns were very welcoming of these men as they believed that this was the only way of being spared from the gruesome disease that was spreading. In the early days, it was also a welcome change to the very mundane lives that they lived. As the disease began to strike closer to home, people began to see the men as one of the last possible ways of being saved from their sins.

The popularity of flagellation began to pose a direct challenge to the Church. Many of the men offering the service had decided to provide it without any approval or authority from the Church. Because they were beginning to gain in popularity (and the Church was losing the respect and awe of the people), these men were seen to be a direct challenge to the Church. The following year as the number of deaths began to slow, the belief that sins could be purged through flagellation quickly went out of favor, and the practice all but ceased.

Flagellants (the men who would flog people to help purge their sins and show their sincere repentance) are commonly seen as fanatics. The teachings of the Church that people should repent was taken several steps further, and it was welcomed because it offered some type of solution to the people, even if it did not work. It was similar to a religious placebo. In some cases, these men actually brought the plague to the towns that they visited, sealing the fate of many. This was obviously in direct opposition to what they were trying to provide. On the other hand, they also provided a service that helped people to cope, to feel that they were doing something to either prevent the spread of the plague or to prepare their soul for the next life. Given the fact that no one could actually explain the cause, this was the most that the large percentage of the population could do.

Scapegoats of the Plague

In addition to killing a large percentage of the people who contracted it, the Black Death inspired people to kill others. Though this should have been in direct opposition to the teachings of Christ, there were still a few people who sought to take advantage of the tragedy spreading throughout Europe.

As has happened repeatedly in European history, one of the primary scapegoats was the Jewish population. Since the Church did not have an adequate explanation for the problem, they and others in power began to blame the Jewish people in their towns and cities, claiming that there was a conspiracy to spread the plague across Europe. Forced confessions were presented in the legal system in which it was claimed that important figures in the Jewish community admitted to putting poison in their water sources. There are even records of some of these legal proceedings that survive today, and they show just how far the people in power would go to place blame on prominent Jewish members.

It is believed that the movement to blame the Jewish population for the Black Death began in Spain and southern France. It is estimated that of the 2.5 million Jewish people in Europe, a third lived in this region, and they had a substantial amount of wealth. Not only were these members of the population more affluent (creating substantial jealousy because of their money and power), they were largely educated. Between their very different economic and social standings and their religious beliefs, they were a fairly easy target. Those who wanted more power could use the idea that the Jewish people were conspiring against Christians so that those in power could steal their money and lands. The peasants and uneducated still saw the Jewish people as the people who killed their savior, and they probably believed that the same people would have no problem killing Christians.

The Jewish population became a completely different kind of victim of the time. During 1348, Aragon's King Peter initiated violent suppression of the Jewish people in Barcelona. At least 20 people were killed, and their homes were pillaged, two teachings that were clearly condemned by the Christ that the king proclaimed to follow. Riots broke out in other cities around Spain, and more members of the Jewish community were killed and their property stolen in the name of appeasing the Christian God. Jewish people living in Spain did have their own places where they could flee to within the country, providing them with protection from the violence perpetrated against them.

Jewish people in other parts of Europe were treated just as poorly but did not have as much power or protection, despite the attempts of others in power. In Naples, Queen Joanna tried to help alleviate some of the wrongs committed against the Jewish community, but her officials were expelled by the people from the towns where those officials were supposed to enforce the taxes.

Even the Pope was unable to provide adequate protection. On July 6th, 1348, Pope Clement VI issued a bull that was meant to apply to all of western Europe. Ultimately, it only ended up protecting the Jewish community in Avignon and its surrounding areas. The people in much of the rest of Europe believed the propaganda which was put forth in part by minor lords and rulers who sought more power and wealth.

All over Europe, the Jewish people were persecuted because it was one of the few explanations that was provided for the unfathomable disaster that claimed lives all over Europe. Of course, some people were taking advantage of the tragedy, but a far greater number of people believed that the Jewish people were intentionally spreading the illness, despite the lack of evidence. Just as they were welcoming of Flagellants who came to punish them for their own guilt, the people believed in the guilt of another group of people. There was no real rhyme or reason to what they would believe; as long as someone was being punished, the people felt like something was being done. Despite how contradictory it was to believe both in their own guilt and the guilt of an entire people of a specific religion, the people of Europe were desperate for a cause. With the Church utterly failing to provide a cause, solution, or even adequate comfort, the people quickly began to lose faith in the teachings they had previously believed without question. The persecution of the Jewish community all over Europe was simply compounding the initial tragedy with another kind that showed some of the worst of humanity.

Plague Doctors

Plague doctors are one of the few symbols from this time period that has survived. They have appeared in video games (such as *Assassin's Creed II*), television, movies, and other types of media. While the vast majority of people who could flee did, the doctors were among the few who actually tried to provide practical scientific services that could minimize the spread and ease the suffering.

Unlike doctors today, their primary job was not to cure patients, although they did try when families became desperate enough for their services. Plague doctors typically spent their time roaming the streets and recording information about the dead. Towns and cities would pay for them to be there, so most plague doctors would treat anyone they encountered who was ill. Some of them did have medical training, but there was no one in Europe who understood the cause, let alone was able to provide any real protection against the Black Death. If a plague doctor was called in, it frequently was as a last-ditch effort to save someone's life. In the rare case that someone survived the disease, it really was more luck or a strong immune system than anything the plague doctor had done.

In addition to working to record the number of people who had died and some basic information about the victims, plague doctors would sometimes be asked to provide autopsies on the dead. The primary purpose for using a plague doctor for this service was to have legal documentation of a death necessary for legal purposes, such as wills. Some doctors used their position to extort money from their patients. However, it is difficult to imagine that was the primary motivator for many. It was an incredibly high-risk profession, with a significant number of plague doctors dying since they were constantly exposed to the dead. In addition to an incredibly high mortality rate for their profession, they were seen as a pariah wherever they went. Their role was so entwined with death that today people can recognize them without much information about their role during the Black Death. Their role came with a certain amount of prestige because they were willing to go into places where others refused to go and to interact with those on their deathbed. Their role was both critical and strange during one of the darkest times in European history, and it has been ingrained into the minds of Europeans even to this day. This has led to plague doctors being connected closely with death, despair, and hope centuries after they first began their morbid work.

Chapter 6 – The Ultimate Equalizer

Following the failure of the Church to provide an adequate explanation for the disease that was destroying so many lives, the deaths of people who were in high standing and positions of power soon began to prove that the problem was not just for the common people. Initially, the problem was easily explained as being something that would only affect people in port cities. Then it became a problem for those who fraternized with people with compromised morals.

With the progression of time, it soon became obvious that the illness went beyond anyone's understanding. High members of the Church succumbed to the disease, proving that either they were corrupt or that the Church did not actually understand the cause. Monarchs who claimed a divine right of the people became victims, proving that they did not have the divine protection they claimed for themselves. In the face of the plague, no one was immune. It was one of the first instances of death being an equalizer that Europe had experienced in centuries, and this was difficult for many people to accept, particularly since many of them were aware of its progression toward Europe. They did not expect it to reach their lands, and even if it did, they believed that their resources and status would save them.

How the Wealthy and Powerful Sought to Escape the Inevitable

The wealthy and powerful felt that they should have been able to escape the grasp of the Black Death. With all of their money, they should have been able to go somewhere that death could not find them. The problem was that there was no such place. By the time people knew that they had contracted it, everyone around them may have been exposed. Even if they had the bubonic plague, the prevalence of fleas and other pests made it difficult to escape the disease. That did not mean they didn't try.

Pope Clement VI kept his place in Avignon smoky so that the air did not smell of the plague and any potential problem associated with the air would be killed by the smoke. He was one of many people who believed that the smell of the plague could make a person sick, not understanding that it was the airborne particles that were the problem. The smell of smoke was not pleasant, but he believed it would ward off the disease that killed so many. While it is obvious today that this method was not the reason he did not contract the disease, it was a far more progressive way of trying to avoid the affliction than some of the attempts by other people in positions of power.

The most successful method was implemented in a few select cities by people who were even more forward thinking. Quarantines will be covered in a future chapter because they were not solely implemented by the rich and powerful. However, it was the people in higher positions who were able to implement and enforce the strict control that kept the plague from either entering or leaving a city or town.

Most people who had the ability to flee did, but that did not always turn out as well as they had hoped. One of the best depictions of this flawed logic was described centuries later by Edgar Allan Poe. His short story "The Masque of the Red Death" was inspired by the inability to escape the Black Death. His story is a work of fiction, but the ideas and problems that the people face in the story reflect how hard some people tried to escape death only to find that there was nowhere to go. Death did not target any one type of social group, class, gender, race, or religion. It could not be negotiated with or bribed. Trying to flee from it proved to be nearly as ineffective.

The Shame of Divine Rights

Many of those who attained a crown had gained their positions through being related to someone who had claimed the throne through blood and trickery. Some of them firmly believed that their God had ordained them the rightful ruler because of their lineage. One obvious sign that they did not fully believe that lie is the amount of infighting that occurred over the centuries, with family members killing each other off to claim thrones all over Europe.

One of the problems that they did not consider as being a threat to their role as monarch was the Black Death. Even as it spread across Europe, many people on thrones believed that it could not possibly affect them. After all, the biggest threats to royalty were other members of royalty. The Black Death would soon prove that there were other aspects in the world that could call into question the belief that any human was placed on a throne because of a divine right to be there. If their God had meant for them to have that role, they should have been allowed to continue in it for a natural lifespan (or until a family member killed them). This was no longer guaranteed once the plague began to claim them.

The Death of a Queen, Princess, and King

The people who claimed that they had the divine right to rule should have been immune from the plague based on their claims. The Black

Death proved this to be the sham that it was, though it would take a few more centuries for the lower classes to start calling royalty out in any meaningful way. What it did do was expose the fundamental problems that the royalty had worked so hard to make people forget as they passed their titles down through the generations.

Though the records are not as well kept, it is believed that the Black Death took members of several royal families. The queen consort to Pedro IV, the king of Aragon, died, as well as one of their daughters and one of his nieces. All three females died within a six-month span.

However, one of the most notable deaths was that of a king. Not much of Alfonso XI of Castile was documented, so historians today do not have much information on what happened during his lifetime. Born in 1311 or 1312 (records vary), he was only an infant when his father, Ferdinand IV of Castile, died. His kingdom was ruled by regents until he became an adult in 1325.

There were definitely several military conflicts that occurred during his reign. He did believe that there had been a decline in chivalry, and he sought to restore what he saw as proper behavior through reforms. He sought to make several other key changes through reform during his reign. Some of his reforms were popular and consolidated his power. As king, he extended the reach of his realm to the Strait of Gibraltar. This showed that he could command and control his military forces. His son, the future King Peter, would be much more ruthless, and by 1350, there seemed to be a power struggle growing in the country.

Then the king fell ill in March of 1350. Sources say that he had become one more victim of the Black Death.

The Beauty and Brains of France

One of the most unfortunate casualties of a royal family member occurred in France. King Philip VI spent a large portion of his time fighting wars and on other types of campaigns, leaving his wife behind to rule the country. His wife, Queen Jeanne la Boiteuse, proved to be more than adequate in her role as his replacement. France not only managed to survive without its king, but it seemed to thrive. She was more than capable as a regent in his absence, and people saw her as the real ruler because she was the one who was present to tend to the country. Then in December of 1349, she began to show signs of having contracted the unthinkable. But the signs were clear, and she did not survive a week after her symptoms presented themselves.

Over the next century, the plague would begin again, and it would upend the royal lines throughout Europe.

Two Birds with One Stone – The Difficulty of Filling the Role of Archbishop of Canterbury

Among the most unnerving instances of what would come to be perceived as the failings of the Church was the death of some of the highest-ranking clergy members. During the 14th century, England was still part of the same church that existed on the continent (Henry VIII would not rule for nearly another 200 years, and it was during his reign that England split from the Catholic Church), so the English clergy was part of the larger organization of the Christian religion on the continent. The Church had experienced substantial turmoil over the last century, and after the death of the last pope (Boniface VIII), the French had managed to gain more power, taking some of the religious power away from Rome. For example, the majority of cardinals who assumed power after Boniface VIII's death were French. They attempted to create their own religious seat in France and to place the next pope in the Avignon Palace.

The power struggle in the Church was still very much a problem during the 1340s. With so many members of the clergy in power being French, they held a lot of sway over many other nations. Thomas Bradwardine was an English clergyman who traveled to Avignon to visit Pope Clement VI. Bradwardine was to be blessed as the Archbishop of Canterbury. During his time in France, Bradwardine had spent a considerable amount of time traveling on foot and by horse around the country taking in the sights and culture. Since he was to assume the greatest position of power within the Church in his country, Bradwardine was networking and making connections to help him during future endeavors.

Bradwardine was well aware that he had not been the first choice for the role of the Archbishop of Canterbury. Despite Bradwardine having been his confessor and close counselor, the English King Edward III had rejected his nomination for the position. Although the exact reason for Edward's rejection of the nomination is not known, it was likely because he was aware that his monks had only made the nomination to please him, not because they felt Bradwardine was qualified (though Bradwardine was more than qualified for the position). The gesture to reject the nomination and to instead approve someone else made the king look magnanimous. Edward III chose John Offord, the man who headed the royal administration. Offord was not qualified for the position, certainly not as qualified as Bradwardine, so the choice raised eyebrows. Still, people did not typically question the king as he was said to be appointed by their God. Before he could receive the pope's blessing, Offord contracted the plague and died in 1349.

With Offord dead, Bradwardine received the king's approval and left for France to receive the blessing his predecessor did not live to receive. Just as the monks who had elected Bradwardine did not stop the election of Offord, now Pope Clement VI could not reject Bradwardine. Essentially, popes had to bless whomever the king appointed. This was how they were able to retain so much power over the centuries, and two centuries later, the insistence of the popes to have things their way would result in the Church splitting again. During the 14th century, they still worked to keep a balance, so they consecrated nearly anyone the kings chose. As Clement VI himself said, no matter whom the king sent, he would agree to the appointment, even if the king chose a jackass.

Unlike other men chosen for the highest religious position in England, Bradwardine was incredibly qualified. He had actually served the Church for years and knew how things should be run. It is strange that the pope chose to make fun of the appointment by bringing a jackass ridden by a clown into the feast that followed the consecration. In jest, the clown sought an appointment for the jackass for the archbishop position.

Following the celebrations, Bradwardine left to return to England. He sought an audience with the king, as was the tradition of the new archbishop following his consecration. Two days after he landed in Dover, he left to begin his work in Rochester. The morning after he arrived in the diocese, the new Archbishop of Canterbury became ill with a fever. Initially, it was thought that the 49-year-old was simply fatigued from all of his travels. By that evening though, the buboes began to show, the first signs that the new archbishop would not hold his position for long. It took five days, but on August 26th, the new archbishop succumbed to the disease he had contracted while in France.

Despite the high risks of keeping a body contaminated by the plague above ground, many of the people who knew him insisted that the archbishop's body be interred in Canterbury where he never had a chance to fulfill his role. It was a 20-mile trip that had to be made using a horse-drawn carriage with a corpse that was marked by the most dangerous and terrifying disease of the time. This shows how highly he was considered by his English peers, particularly after the less than friendly reception in France. He had not only been a respected member of the clergy, but he also had considerable political power and was adept at numerous aspects of the isle's politics.

This proved that the disease could take down even the most well-respected and apparently upright members of the Church. What made Bradwardine's death even more devastating was that it followed the death of an English princess. The next chapter covers the loss that preceded the tragic death of the new archbishop, but his death was what really emphasized how little the Church understood about the disease that was killing people all over the continent.

Chapter 7 – Stealing the Future – Princess Joan

While there were many larger than life figures that became victims of the Black Death, there was one person who remains an example of just how cruel the disease was. It did not care about who a person was, their social status, or their age. It was a devastating disease that would steal the present and future for many people. Few deaths of powerful figures were more shocking and tragic than that of Princess Joan of England.

The life of a noblewoman, particularly one in a royal family, was already difficult. They were not expected to toil in the fields like women of other classes, but their future was not exactly bright either. Their fathers chose who they would marry. Once married, their main purpose was to produce heirs for their husbands. Unlike today, the average lifespan of a woman of a higher station was less than that of her husband. Most of them would die in childbirth.

Still, the arranged marriage of the daughter of the king of England showed promise for at least being amicable. Princess Joan's father loved her, and though the marriage was definitely a political move, it appeared that he had chosen a prince who wanted to make his daughter comfortable (at the very least). There was a lot of promise for the futures of both England and Castile as the two countries planned to marry their children together. It was just one more way that the plague altered the history of the continent.

King Edward III and a World at War

To better understand the significance of the arranged marriage of Princess Joan, it is important to know about the world that her father created. Princess Joan was the daughter of one of the most notable English kings in European history, King Edward III. The son of King Edward II and Isabella of France, not much is known about Edward's childhood after his birth in 1312. The first major event of his life occurred in 1327 when he was 14 or 15 years old. His mother and Roger Mortimer (her lover) successfully deposed his father, installing Edward III as the king. Together, the queen consort and her lover acted as the rulers because the new king was clearly too young to manage a kingdom. A year after he was installed as the king, Edward married Philippa of Hainault. The lovers' reign ended just three years after they took power in 1330. King Edward III was now 18, and like his mother, he was not afraid to act. Mortimer was executed, and he banished his mother from his court.

Edward III was one of the most adept monarchs of his time and in his long-ruling house. He belonged to the House of Plantagenet that included many of the most notable monarchs in British history. The dynasty descended from Geoffrey V of Anjou, whose son, Henry II, became King of England in 1154. The House of Plantagenet would last until 1485, 108 years after the death of Edward III. The last of the Plantagenets was King Richard III, who was famously villainized by William Shakespeare, who worked to please the monarchs of his time which belonged to the incredibly memorable House of Tudor. Prior to the rise of the House of Tudor and Henry VIII, King Edward

III was one of the most ruthless and charismatic rulers in English history.

At the time, England had claimed lands in France, but the territories that belonged to England were frequently disputed by the king of France. At 28 years old, King Edward III began to fight for the lands that he claimed in France. Taking the title of King of France in 1340, the English king began one of the most infamous wars in European history—the Hundred Years' War. France, however, had their own king, and he fought against Edward III during the early years of the war. This war was not continuous, and there were years when there was little or no fighting. However, the reason that the war began would not be settled until over a century later.

Edward brought his son Edward, commonly referred to as the Black Prince, to Normandy to fight for his claimed lands. They were successful in driving the French from Crecy and then took the port city of Calais. His son had earned his moniker because of his armor, and many believed that he had a black heart because of his ferocity on and off the field. However, the Black Prince would never reach the throne. He would die about a year before his father, who would finally die in 1377.

Edward III was like a scourge to many of the people who lived in the French countryside as his mercenaries and fighters frequently roamed and took what they needed or wanted. His methods are certainly seen as cruel and despotic today. However, for this period of time, Edward III was seen as one of the most chivalrous and constitutionally driven monarchs because he did adhere to the constitutions that his father and grandfather had either helped to forge or were forced to accept. Given the fact that his father was a weak ruler (as he was deposed by his wife and her lover), Edward III certainly could have felt that the strings put on his father could have been ignored. As a strong ruler, it would not have been entirely surprising if Edward III decided to ignore the agreements of his predecessors with the English people (particularly the nobles). But he did not, instead honoring those agreements and requirements nearly to the letter. Naturally, this king nearly always got what he wanted, but compared to many other rulers of his time, he at least appeared to adhere to the rules set before him. Much of the way we see him today can be attributed to the evolution in thinking about what a ruler should be, and applying that thinking retroactively does not leave any ruler looking particularly good. Having started the Hundred Years' War, King Edward III was very much a fighter, but he was also a product of his time and a dynasty notorious for either being ruthless or inept. There were very few in House of Plantagenet who were not on one extreme or the other of the spectrum.

Edward III had 13 children. With the population of England being about a third of France's, victory would require more than just military prowess; the king needed to leverage his children to make alliances that could help him keep what he had won and ensure future successful campaigns. His daughter, Princess Joan, was betrothed to Peter of Castile, the son of one of the most powerful monarchs in Europe (Alfonso XI) in 1345 when she was just 11 or 12 years old. The alliance would have set the stage for the eventual merging of England, Wales, France, and Castile.

When she was 15, Princess Joan and a large retinue traveled from England to marry her fiancé. Her father was always planning for the future, and that included plans for his dynasty long after his death. However, he was not simply using his daughter to further the claims of his family; it would appear later that he did indeed love his daughter. It is very possible that he treated his children much better than his parents seemed to have treated him, and he was not the monster to them that he would be considered to be by those whom he fought against.

Preparing for a Celebration

The marriage of the 15-year-old Princess Joan was seen as both a significant event and a distraction from the war and pestilence that had descended on the lands. Today, 15 is certainly seen as too young for marriage, but it was a common age for marriage during the Dark

Ages. Women in royal families rarely outlived their husbands, frequently dying in childbirth or from infections after the birth of a child. Joan's life expectancy would have been about 30 years, so she was already essentially middle-aged. With the queen's primary purpose being to produce children, and pregnancy being a huge risk to both the women and children, it was important for a princess to wed as young as possible while her body was more resilient and she had more time to produce as many children as her body could handle.

Doubtless, the marriage was a calculated event to further Edward III's lineage, but it was also a festive time. The king sent a very large retinue with his daughter to both protect her and to help make her comfortable as she began her new life. Much was written about her trip from Portsmouth, England, to Bordeaux, France. To afford his daughter every luxury, the procession included a portable chapel. This would help to keep her from mixing with the more common people in the local churches. She would be attended by the most notable priest in Bordeaux, Gerald de Podio. He would manage all of her spiritual needs leading up to the wedding. Minstrels accompanied her, including Prince Pedro's favorite. He had intended for his favorite minstrel to help his future wife become better acquainted with the music and customs of his lands (her future home). It shows an interesting connection in that the future king was trying even before the wedding to create a better future for his bride.

More importantly, she had a heavy protective guard. Considering his reputation in parts of France and the fact that some of the regions where the retinue would travel were hot spots for criminals, the king had sent over 100 bowmen to accompany his daughter. This did include men who had fought with him during his victory in Crecy. Having those warriors included in the wedding party would have also been a reminder to the king of France of his own failings so that he did not attempt to attack them. He certainly would have watched in horror, knowing that he could not stop the marriage between his

English and Castilian rivals. It would have been a very dark day for the French monarchy if things had gone differently.

Her wedding dress was a luxurious gown of red velvet. Jewels and diamonds were added to the gown and other clothing that she was to wear prior to the wedding. The wealth and riches sent with his daughter essentially required their own ship. This served two purposes. First, he was showing his own wealth to the new in-laws. Second, it was meant to show his daughter that he loved her and that he would not spare any expense for what should have been one of the most memorable days of her life.

Everything was set as she traveled south where her wedding was to be held. As her retinue reached Bordeaux, everything seemed to be going as planned. The bride-to-be had a wedding gown that would be the envy of those who saw it. She traveled in comfort, and the people around her seemed to honestly care for her well-being. Unfortunately, the timing could not have been worse as her retinue arrived around the same time that the Black Death finally reached Bordeaux. Despite being warned upon their arrival, the party felt a false sense of security. Whether that was because of their station or because England had not yet seen the full horrors of the plague, it was a warning that they learned too late should have been heeded.

A Matter of Timing – Celebration Turns to Tragedy

The princess arrived with her enormous retinue in August of 1348. As she and three of her most important officials were escorted by the mayor, he sought to make them as comfortable as possible. They were to spend their time in the Chateau de l'Ombrière, a castle that had been constructed by the Plantagenets and overlooked the estuary. In passing, the mayor mentioned that the plague had been creating issues for the people of Bordeaux. Seemingly removed from the problem, this was likely seen as a misfortune that posed no issues to Princess Joan's retinue beyond perhaps causing issues with the food or other minor details.

In truth, the Black Death was already claiming a large portion of the population of Bordeaux. The corpses of victims piled up in the streets and near the docks, creating a very macabre scene. Despite the warning from the mayor that the plague was beginning to become a more significant problem, the wedding party continued with their plans. It seemed of little consequence to them that the lower classes suffered because the plague was not thought to be a direct threat to them.

Unfortunately, the chateau was close to one of the locations where corpses were being dumped. Rats, pests, and pets had a veritable feast at the docks and then very possibly made a trip into the chateau to eat what they could find among the scraps left by the large wedding party. Set up in an area that was so close to the plague, the wedding party really did not stand a chance.

One of the first to fall ill and die was her advisor, Robert Bourchier. Princess Joan probably watched in horror as many in her retinue began to fall ill, and their bodies became horrific reminders that no one was immune. The first major member of her party died on August 20th. Less than two weeks later, Joan herself fell ill. She died on September 2nd, although some authors place her death on July 1st. Word was immediately sent to her father, and he learned on October 1st of the death of his daughter and with her his future plans for his lineage. His other daughter to reach adulthood had already been married to an English lord to strengthen his ties at home.

Edward III then had the task of letting King Alfonso XI of Castile know what had happened as his daughter had journeyed toward her new home. His letter still survives today and shows that he actually felt real sorrow for her loss, not just because it had destroyed his plans for the future. As ruthless as he was as a king, he was a human (as he points out in his letter), and the loss of his child seemed to have struck him pretty hard. He released King Alfonso XI from the marriage agreement, allowing him to find another bride for his son.

What happened with the princess's body is not documented. Given the extent of the deaths caused by the Black Death, it is almost certain that her body was burned along with many of the other victims. Strangely, the body of Bourchier was sent back to England where he was buried. However, he was the first notable victim, and the wedding party must have thought that they had the luxury of time. Such contact with his body would have helped further spread the plague within the party. By the time the princess died, the plague had already swept through most of them, leaving a much smaller group of people to tend to her body. Her father did seek to have her body brought home. After he learned of Joan's death, Edward III paid far more than was necessary to one of his bishops to go and retrieve her body so that she could be buried close to home. It is unknown what happened, but it is almost certain that the bishop did not retrieve the body. The burial of the princess would have been recorded along with other notable events of the time, but there are no records of it. The bishop could have decided it was too risky and hid during the time when he was supposed to be gone. Perhaps he did make the attempt but was understandably unsuccessful. By the time the king paid him, it was the end of October, nearly two months since she had died. The people of Bordeaux would not have allowed a plague corpse to remain unburied or unburned for such a long period of time anyways. This is the most likely scenario as the port town took extreme measures as the plague continued to claim lives. They actually began to burn the corpses of plague victims, resulting in a fire that got out of control and burned significant portions of the residences and homes near the port. This included the chateau where Joan had been staying. By the time the bishop arrived, there would have been no body left to take home.

Undoubtedly, the death of Princess Joan would have been seen as fortunate by the French king. The threat of an alliance between two of his largest rivals was dissolved, apparently by divine intervention.

The Black Prince and others of the Plantagenet line would seek to take parts of Spain by force, but no further marriage alliance was successful with Castile.

To King Edward III, the threat of the plague became much more obvious. Having lost his daughter to it, he became far more conscious of the potential risks of the disease. Now fully aware of just how devastating and quickly the disease claimed lives, he and the Black Prince would leave the heavily populated city of London for a small home in the countryside when the plague reached England. By the time the Archbishop of Canterbury died of the disease the next year, the king was already acutely aware of the risks and was taking as many precautions as he could to secure the rest of his family from the effects.

The loss of his daughter would eventually also lead to a more compassionate understanding of the plague. King Edward III had a mass burial site established for victims of the Black Death. Of course, there were certainly practical aspects to this, but there were not many rulers who actively worked to provide a place of interment on consecrated grounds. Just two years after Joan's death, Edward III bought and established a plague cemetery close to the Tower of London. He then established a chapel that he dedicated to the Virgin Mary.

This level of care might seem at odds with the merciless monarch that many think of today when talking about Edward III. He was a monarch of a very different time that followed very different rules. Having seen his father be deposed by his mother, he was more than likely a puppet of her whims for three years as another man assumed his father's place. This undoubtedly helped to set the stage for the man he would become. By 1350, he had successfully established himself as a powerful monarch in Europe but at a high cost. The loss of his daughter would have been felt on a very personal level and not just for the politics. He was apparently a better parent to his children than his ineffective father and cruel mother. The death of Joan made him much more compassionate to those who suffered the same fate.

Very aware that he could have easily become a victim, or could have lost his life in any of his military campaigns, there was much for the king to be thankful for on that day in 1350 when he and the rest of his family did not fall ill. The people who brought word of her death could have been carriers, bringing the plague literally right to him. His gratitude for being spared would certainly wane considerably over the next few years as the plague appeared to cease to be a threat, but he would occasionally increase the money provided for the upkeep of the cemetery and chapel he had established. As he lay dying in 1377, he finally made good on the promises he made earlier for the lands and established services dedicated to the plague victims, showing that as he lay dying, the death of his daughter still likely was on his mind. As he believed he would go see her in the next life, perhaps he felt he needed to fulfill his promise.

Chapter 8 – Decline of the Catholic Church and the Rise of Mysticism

The initial belief in the Catholic Church quickly began to wane after the effects of the Black Death showed no signs of stopping. As people followed the instructions of their priests, they had hoped that things would begin to improve. It was easy to believe that they had perhaps strayed from the path ordained by their God, so atonement should have resulted in Him being appeased.

Instead of their world becoming more stable, the plague continued to spread. It moved from the coastal towns and ports inland, killing the people living in the towns that dotted the landscape. The fact that their local clergy were not spared caused people to begin to question the Church that instructed them in their daily lives. If the clergy who served their vengeful God were not spared, then the problem clearly went beyond the sins of a few people.

Then, major religious and political figures began to succumb to the gruesome death that was supposed to be a punishment for the people who were immoral. As people saw major figures who were supposedly ordained by their God dying, it was clear that the Church did not have the solution to the pestilence spreading over the land. Since they could no longer believe in the Church to produce a real cause or solution for the Black Death, people began to look elsewhere for the answers.

Life Before the Black Death

As previously detailed, the people of the 14th century were largely living in agrarian societies. The land was owned by the monarchs, the nobility, and the clergy. It was assumed that their rise to power was a sign of the approval of the Christian God. Since the vast majority of the European population struggled to live day to day and were largely uneducated, they believed what those from the higher stations said. They were forced into wars for which the commoners gained nearly nothing, and they were subject to the whims of those who owned the land. Bandits, marauders, and mercenaries roamed the land along with tax collectors. All of these groups plied their trade through violence to get what they thought they were owed or deserved.

Through all of the misery, the Church provided the hope for something better if the people simply lived according to God's will. If they could put up with the misery in this life, a better life awaited them. After all, Jesus had promised that the meek would inherit the earth, and there was no one as meek as the people who worked the fields and managed the livestock. The promise of something better was enough to help them be complacent. Their lords provided some protection, and they were able to feed themselves most of the time. Famine, war, and illness would occasionally make life almost unbearable, but those incidents were typically short-lived, leaving enough people to begin rebuilding the society again.

As towns grew, there also came the hope of a better life before death. People began to realize that there was more money and opportunity if they became merchants, servants to the nobility, or sailors. There were risks, but typically the risks were not that much worse than the ones they faced as farmers and shepherds. This drew an increasing number of people into the towns, leaving some of the fields with fewer workers. Before the Black Death, things were getting more difficult for the people clinging to the agrarian way of life, but life was still manageable. Those whose families found success in the towns which were able to provide far more money than if they had remained behind to help with the work in the fields and with livestock. The people who were willing to risk death on the seas or abroad stood to gain the most, and many of the most fortunate or savvy businessmen were able to change their class as port towns grew. The trading business offered something new— goods that had not been seen on the continent for a long time. With people migrating to these ports, there were a growing number of merchants, increasing the demands for foreign goods.

However, life was still difficult. The conditions in towns were terrible (and a large contributing factor to the easy spread of the Black Death). Sanitation practices had substantially declined in the majority of Europe after the fall of Rome, and the people rarely bathed, and their waste was discarded all over the towns and cities. People bathed in bodies of water, and if those bodies were downstream from where towns and cities were discarding plague corpses, it was exacerbating the problem. The homes were small and not very secure, and it was difficult to live in cramped quarters. The people had always been taught by the Church that if they wanted to plan for their future in heaven, they had to put up with the misery in the here and now to sow better rewards later; in other words, after their death. Now they had a chance to reap the benefits during their lifetime instead of after they had died. It was attractive, and they withstood the discomfort and problems of the living conditions because there was the promise of something better soon.

Then the Black Death reached their shores, and everything changed.

Prestige Lost

As the plague entered Europe and began to spread, the people could easily be persuaded that it was the lives that they lived that had caused the problem. They had sought to better their lives at the expense of that other life after death, or they had not followed the Church's teachings as they should. They had sinned in their minds if not with their bodies. All of these were the excuses that the Church said had caused the plague to finally reach their lands.

As entire towns died because of the plague, including members of the clergy, it became obvious that the Church did not have the answers. Not only were their explanations inadequate, but their solutions did nothing to slow the plague stretching across the continent at an unimaginable rate. The fact that a person would be dead within a week of contracting the illness meant that there was no time to adequately put their lives in order before they died. The clergy sought to save themselves instead of helping their congregations. Because they were too scared for their own lives, priests began to refuse to provide last rites for the plague victims. This would have been a huge blow to the people as their immortal souls were their last hope for a better life, and it was now being denied them. Even the priests who did remain at their posts and provided the essential services could only provide temporary comfort.

To try to demonstrate that the Church was compassionate to their plight, Pope Clement VI tried to assuage fears by granting the remission of sins for anyone who died of the Black Death. A person who was dying could confess to another person who was not a member of the clergy for absolution, even if the only available person was a woman. While it certainly could have had an effect in the early days of the plague, by the time the pope offered this small consolation, the number of victims was astounding. Since the way that a body was managed after death was also heavily dictated by the

Church, those who had died were absolved but still could not go to heaven since their bodies were not properly handled. Instead of burying individuals with the traditional ceremony, plague victims were dumped into mass graves, which were not authorized and went against the Church's teachings of a proper burial. The Church could offer no solution and did not heed the concerns of the people, as it was impossible to bury all of the victims in individual graves. There were not enough clergy available for the tasks, even if they had all been willing. They remained largely silent about the practice of mass burials instead of condemning the practice (as they likely would have if the plague had not been so widespread).

Fearing for their own lives, the people continued to use mass graves. More concerned with survival than a future existence, they chose to try to rid the towns and cities of the dead. Ignoring the teachings of the Church that had been an integral part of their lives, the people felt mass graves provided the best means of survival. The Church had already proved it had no idea what was happening or how to stem it, so the people would not have listened even if the Church had spoken out against the practice. To the people, if the Church had been so wrong about burials, there were many other aspects of their faith to question. They began to wonder what other things the Church had gotten wrong. For now, they had a far more pressing problem.

It became obvious to people that the solution did not lie in the Church that had been the backbone of their belief for centuries. But if not the Church, where would they turn?

The Rise of Uncertainty and Strange Beliefs

The Flagellant Movement was just one of the many strange sets of beliefs that people embraced during the Black Death. Though they had lost faith in their Church, most people still believed that the plague was a punishment from their God—it was just clear that the Church was a part of the problem and not part of the solution. Since the clergy could not produce answers and solutions, people began to turn to mysticism and strange means to satisfy their God's vengeance. They had to win forgiveness through any means possible.

Self-harm or accepting physical punishment was one way to do this. Targeting the minorities and blaming them was another. However, neither of these ideas provided an adequate cause for the widespread problem, nor a solution that was obviously yielding results. People began to believe more in superstition and fatalism, which created an entirely different set of problems. Small pockets of people who followed more apocalyptic ideas of the world began to increase, thinking the world was ending.

Not all of the people gave up hope, believing that whatever happened was fated to happen. In addition to the persecution of the Jewish community (and to a lesser extent other smaller minority groups), these small pockets began to talk of social reforms and much larger changes. They stopped listening to the Church's teachings, as well as the decrees of their monarchs and lords. As already mentioned, some figures did try to protect the Jewish population, but anti-Semitism had a strong hold on the people, and those people no longer believed in the authority figures in power. This stretched beyond the treatment of other people though. The once complacent population was no longer willing to heed the words of a Church that had clearly failed them. There was a new malcontent with their lot that would only be made worse in the years following the initial wave of the Black Death as the Church continued to fail them.

The Church Loses Its Way

Once the fear of the Black Death began to subside, the Church was faced with the task of finding new priests to act for them. With a decimated population, they had far fewer options. Having to select from a much smaller pool, the requirements to be a priest or man of the Church were relaxed. Uneducated men were welcomed into the profession and were given minimal training so that they could go out to help tend the flock that had become lost during the plague years. The fact that these men clearly knew less and were less capable than the priests and other clergy prior to the plague meant that the people were less inclined to trust them.

Perhaps the worst thing that people noticed about the Catholic Church as Europe tried to cope with the aftermath of the plague was that the higher-ranking officials were getting richer. Entire towns were wiped out, and money was needed to help start rebuilding them. Instead of putting their money into helping the people, the Church was hoarding it. The clergy were taking advantage of the tragedy to accumulate wealth and centralize power. This was perhaps one of the greatest blows to the Church as an increasing number of people no longer were willing to trust them as they had in the days before the Black Death. The Church had gained wealth from those who had died, which went against everything it had taught the people. Now, the people were beginning to see how the Church worked because it was exposed to far more transparency than it had been in the centuries before the plague.

Ultimately, the Black Death planted the seeds of discontentment with the Church. Instead of being seen as a way for salvation, it was increasingly described as a corrupt institution. Less than 150 years later, the doubt sowed by the Black Death would come to a head as Martin Luther nailed his *Ninety-five Theses* to a church door, beginning the Reformation.

Chapter 9 – Art of the Black Death

The Black Death both inspired and destroyed the arts of the day. Because the pandemic touched the lives of almost everyone on an entire continent, all of the art of the time reflected just how drastically it changed their lives. The Church lost a substantial amount of its power and trust, and as the primary patron of the arts, this played a huge role in how art developed during this time.

Petrarch's Profound Loss

Francesco Petrarca, more commonly known as Petrarch, is the most well-known poet from the 14th century. His most famous work was *Il Canzoniere*, and it contained more than 350 poems. His influence on European literature cannot be overstated. His work has inspired many of the great poets since his death, including Dante and Shakespeare. His works included many of the common themes covered in poetry, but he was perhaps best known for his love poems to a woman he saw in church when he was 23, Laura. In his works, he contemplates many of the questions that men have always asked, questions about mortality and fame, but his works also have a fairly philosophical bent to them as well. Many poets have tried to mimic his style, and they still find inspiration from his words centuries after his death.

Petrarch definitely became famous for his poetry, but that was not the purpose for his works. His poetry was about his own philosophical and mental meanderings through the meaning of life and his profound love for Laura. One of his books even ended with poetry of him hoping to meet with her again after he died. As a philosopher and moralist, his writings went well beyond poetry, and he had a singular interest in saving the works of ancient writers. He began an immense collection of works from writers of the ancient worlds that were far more advanced than the Christian European society of the Middle Ages, and he took many of their ideas to heart. By the time he died in 1374, he had one of the largest private collections of such works in the world.

His philosophies and the valuing of past writers influenced his works, but Petrarch was also personally affected by the Black Death. The love of his life and the center of his poetry, Laura de Noves, died in Avignon, France in 1348, one of the many who succumbed to the disease once it reached the city. His poetry during this time reflects his profound personal loss in a way that most other poets cannot adequately express their own similar sorrows. Most people proclaim to be at a loss for words when such personal tragedy strikes, but he found the words to lament how significantly her death affected his world. Petrarch had first seen her in Avignon in 1327, but when the Black Death visited Avignon, he was in Parma, Italy. In his poetry, he proclaimed "that nothing more ought in this life to please me" once he learned of her death and interment.

His brother, Gherardo, was at a great risk of dying from the Black Death as it reached the monastery in Montrieux, France where he lived. Petrarch wrote to him, perhaps not aware that his brother was already dealing with the ravages of the disease. Petrarch decries the arrival of the Black Death and declares,

> I would, my brother, that I had never been born, or, at least, had died before these times. How will posterity believe that there has been a time when without the lightnings of heaven or the fires of earth, without wars or other visible slaughter, not this or that part of the earth, but well-nigh the whole globe, has remained without inhabitants. When has any such thing been even heard or seen; in what annals has it ever been read that houses were left vacant, cities deserted, the country neglected, the fields too small for the dead and a fearful and universal solitude over the whole earth?

As most people tried to grasp what was happening around them, Petrarch was already thinking in terms of the future and how it would be affected. Naturally, there had been pestilence before on similarly large scales, but Europe had either been largely immune or had completely forgotten them. The scale of death this time around was unimaginable, and there seemed to be no end in sight.

Fortunately, Gherardo survived the Black Death that visited his monastery. In fact, he and his faithful dogs were the only ones who did not die as the plague took the remaining members of the clergy. This was one small relief to Petrarch in what would certainly have seemed like a cataclysmic event. It would also provide some hope for the future because all was not lost.

Boccaccio and *The Decameron*

Another notable writer from the Middle Ages was Giovanni Boccaccio. While Petrarch's works were passionate and overflowed with emotions, Boccaccio wrote in a much more detached and analytical style. The language he used was still artistic, but there was more of an objective feeling to the things he wrote. Petrarch was inspired to write based on his own sense of loss, as well as the loss for the future. He imagined how difficult the effects of the plague would be to overcome and that no one would ever fully comprehend what had happened—if anyone even survived the plague.

Boccaccio was similarly inspired by the events of the Black Death, but his work, *The Decameron*, would become a pillar of literature at the time. It delved into subjects from a more detached point of view as the characters were fictional. It begins with a party of seven men and three women who attempt to escape the Black Death by going to a villa outside of the city where they resided.

While the book itself is a work of fiction, it contains probably what is the most infamous description of exactly how virulent and gruesome the plague was. Boccaccio did not spare the reader from the descriptions of some of the worst elements of the disease. He described the welts that formed, the blackening of the skin, and the blood that seemed to ooze from almost everywhere on the victim. This graphic description has helped scientists and scholars to understand just how horrific the disease was long after the initial introduction of the plague into Europe.

Nor does his work focus solely on the horrors of the physical effects on the people he wrote about. The early portions of *The Decameron* detail the illness and the panic of the people who suffered through it. His work describes the suffering and mental anguish that gripped the city that the main characters would attempt to escape. Finally, his story provides a look into how social order began to fail and the decline of religious traditions as people began to use mass burials to try to survive.

The beginning of the tale is very grim before moving into the events and lives of the main characters once they escaped the city. Unlike Petrarch, Boccaccio did not seem to be religious, or at least he did not invoke religion nearly so often. As Petrarch declared that humans had brought the plague upon themselves for their sins, Boccaccio seemed to be of a more secular mind in his works. He did not lament the fall of man or their having earned the wrath of their God. Instead, he presented a more scientific (and therefore more reliable) look at the disease and its effects.

All of this he provided to posterity under the guise of one of the most famous works of fiction ever produced in Europe.

Fall of the New Siena Movement

The Black Death certainly inspired different kinds of art, but it also stole it. The Siena Movement was just growing in popularity, and new styles of paintings were being developed by the artists who were a part of this movement during the middle of the 14th century. Siena, Italy was a city that was beginning to grow rapidly, and before the arrival of the Black Death, it attracted a number of talented painters. Cathedrals were being constructed and decorated. The art of the time was beginning to reflect this new phase of the city, a sense of style that was unique to the region.

Then the Black Death arrived. There were many great painters who had come to Siena to practice their craft and to refine their techniques, notably Ambrogio and Pietro Lorenzetti. Nearly all of the painters would perish in the city, victims of the plague. The new Sienese school of art was snuffed out before it could fully finish exploring its potential.

Chapter 10 – The First Quarantine and Successful Containment

The Black Death was the first real pandemic to hit Europe since the Justinian Plague over five centuries earlier. The people were at a loss as to how to stop what seemed like a cruel punishment from their God because they had no memory of ever experiencing a disease that could kill so quickly and spread with no apparent rhyme or reason. Some of the port cities had attempted to prevent further entrance of those with the disease, but there were no laws or enforcement that would keep the sick from mixing with those who had not yet been exposed.

Europe had never had any need for far-reaching health measures or the application of public safety prior to the Black Death. They were ill-equipped to manage any kind of pandemic, but they were suddenly forced to try to find ways to minimize exposure. By the time Italy realized that the problem was on a much larger scale than they anticipated, they began to implement and enforce rules in the hopes that it would stem the tide against an unseen enemy that had been winning the battle against humans since it arrived.

Early Attempts

At first, port cities monitored the arrival of ships and sailors looking for signs that more than just cargo had arrived with the passengers. By March of the year after the Black Death arrived (1348), they were starting to force ships to leave if the ships were suspected of carrying people suffering from the highly contagious illness.

This was an admirable early attempt to keep more people who were sick from entering the ports. However, it did not account for the people who were already in the city, nor did it take into account the people who were entering the port towns and cities from the inland routes as well. Still, it did at least mean that diseased people were not coming from abroad, reducing additional waves of the sickness striking the towns through the most obvious way that it could reach the people.

There was also the problem of the ships being allowed to make port at other places where no controls were being implemented. Italy was the first country to try to stop more plague victims from entering. In fact, they were the only country to try to keep sick people from entering their ports. The ships that they turned away moved onto ports in Aragon and France, ensuring that the plague would infect far greater numbers. Had the ships been denied entry to ports in other countries, it is likely that the death toll could have been significantly reduced, although it would also have been a death sentence to all those aboard the vessels.

Venice

Venice was one of the three Italian cities hardest hit at the beginning of the plague (along with Florence and Genoa). As the first place where historians point to as the entry point for the disease, Sicily also suffered during this time, but as an island, there was more of a natural containment mechanism should the people choose to use it. From the three major cities in Italy, the Black Death quickly made progress inland, reaching towns and cities all over the continent that were far removed from those first contaminated ships. It was clear that the people who entered the cities were bringing the disease with them, and the people fleeing from towns and cities were further spreading the disease to areas that would have otherwise been unaffected. It had been determined that the only way to survive was to avoid any contact with humans who had contracted the disease. They were unaware that the pests could also contaminate them, but human interaction was still a major contributor. By keeping the sick out of the cities, they knew that they could significantly stymy the disease.

Venice was one of the first cities to implement a quarantine to prevent further introduction of sick sailors to their city. Realizing that they should not allow some ships to enter, they shut their port from all ship entry without proper measures being implemented first. Any ship that was believed to carry contaminated passengers and sailors was denied entry. All ships that were allowed to enter the city were required to remain in isolation for 30 days, and they also forced travelers to remain in isolation for 30 days. Considering the fact that a person who had the plague typically was dead within a week, 30 days seemed like more than enough time to ensure that all visitors to the city were proven to be clean prior to being allowed to mix with the rest of the populace. This proved to be an incredibly effective method, and one they would come to perfect with each successive wave of the plague that arose. Over time, the number of days for quarantine would become 40 days instead of 30.

A process was also put in place to verify both the point of origin of a ship and the health of those on the ship. The captain of a recently arrived vessel would leave the ship in a lifeboat and head to the magistrate's office. He would be placed into a small enclosure where he would talk at a safe distance from the official. Glass and other protections were put in place to ensure that any captains who were sick could not pass the plague on to the health magistrate. This extra measure was put in place under the misguided belief that breathing the air around someone with the plague would get one sick. In a vague way, they were right as plague in the lungs (pneumonic plague) can release airborne contamination, and the extra precaution did stop the particles and other forms of contact from contaminating the magistrate. The captain would also need to provide written proof of where his ship had been and the health of his crew and other people on his ship (such as passengers). He also had to detail where the goods and items he was bringing to the city originated. If it was suspected that any hints of the plague were present either in the crew or in the cargo, the ship was directed to the quarantine station where it would remain for 30 days (or 40 days a few years after the first quarantine).

Other Italian cities began to adopt this measure of protection as it proved to be one of the best ways of combating the illness for which no other cause could be found besides human contact. By requiring people to remain apart from the city until they had proven that they were not infected, the cities were able to keep the Black Death from annihilating their populace. Trade slowed because of the measures to block the plague from entering, but after the devastation seen in the first few months of the epidemic, it was a trade-off that the people of Venice, then the whole of Italy and then the rest of Europe, was willing to make to ensure that the plague did not continue to cause death on the same scale as the first wave.

Landlocked Efforts

Venice was the first city to practice a type of quarantine, but what they learned could certainly be applied to inland cities. It would certainly be more challenging since there were many ways to enter these cities besides through the gates. However, the precautions did significantly reduce the risk once they were enforced.

By May of 1348, Pistoia (another town in Italy) started to implement similar measures against further plague victims entering their city. The people in power also sought to stop the spread within the city. Laws were enacted that dictated the way people were to live their lives, similar to what the Catholic Church had done prior to the outbreak but with a much more obvious reason and more far-reaching consequences. They placed strict regulations on any goods that were imported and exported, but this did not have the effect that they had hoped. With regulations in place on goods, the population was still not spared. It is estimated that despite the regulations, roughly 70% of the population of Pistoia died.

Milan had enacted its own set of laws around the same time, although they were not identical. In contrast to the Pistoia authorities, those in Milan were far stricter. When they found that a home had a plague victim, the home was sealed so that no one could leave, ensuring that the plague did not leave the home while condemning any of the people who had been inside. This city was spared the same outbreak that killed so many in Pistoia. When the plague again surfaced in 1350, the city of Milan had created a building that was designated a pest house where those sick with the plague and anyone who was tending them would remain in quarantine. This building was safely outside the city walls so that the victims would not have the opportunity to infect the people within the city.

Italy was the first country to implement and enforce any kind of quarantine for many years after the first outbreak. Castile, Aragon, France, and England were painfully slow in adopting similar measures to protect their people. England was so lax in its approach that it would suffer a huge toll during the Great Plague of 1665. They had few to no laws in place for that round of the plague, leaving London and the rest of the country vulnerable to a highly deadly disease that was being effectively limited in continental Europe.

Plague Cemeteries

The more astute members of society began to realize that more could be done with the corpses to ensure that the potential for contamination was minimized. The first plague cemeteries were set up too late for them to be effective, and Venice suffered the loss of tens of thousands of people during the first wave of the plague. In addition to the other quarantine measures they had in place, they did dedicate certain cemeteries for the mass burials of plague victims with each progressive cycle of the detestable disease; there were also more measures put in place to minimize the exposure of the healthy to the victims who died from it. Plague cemeteries would become popular throughout much of Europe, and as already mentioned, Edward III following his daughter's death dedicated a cemetery for the burial of plague victims. It was perhaps the least effective of the quarantines, but it did provide the people with a much faster means of disposing the bodies than a traditional burial. Nor did it create the kinds of problems experienced by Bordeaux, where attempts to burn victims quickly led to uncontrollable fires. It did create other problems, such as providing a dedicated area for rats and other animals to find food, but there was not enough understood about the disease for the people to take the kinds of actions we know to take today.

All of these examples are some of the earliest recorded public health measures in Europe. Other places were practicing similar types of controls, although not everywhere in Europe did so. It took the loss of between a quarter and half of the population of Europe for the people to realize that there were steps they could take to slow or entirely prevent exposure. The plague would continue to return to Europe, particularly during the summers (which drove many of the nobility and monarchs to summer homes). Italy quickly began to take control of the problem, limiting how many people would be exposed. Over time, the other countries would follow their example. As the hub of trade during the 14th and 15th centuries, Italy had a vested interest in containing the problem as early as possible. They were the first country in Europe to suffer the horrors of the Black Death, giving them a good reason to be concerned that it could happen again. Some of their early attempts would be unsuccessful, but ultimately the measures would evolve into the kinds of quarantine that many countries practice today.

Chapter 11 – Beyond the Human Toll

The toll of the Black Death is often considered in terms of human lives lost because it was what people focused on as the plague swept across Europe. What is less well remembered were the other ways that the Black Death affected people both immediately and in the following years after the first wave of the disease.

Animals Affected by the Plague

There were two primary problems with the Black Death in terms of the animals who lived side by side with humans. First, many of the animals were just as susceptible to contracting and dying from the disease as humans. Second, most of the animals were not companions to people, so the loss of animals at this time compounded the impossibly high death toll by reducing the amount of available food and clothing.

Losing Food and Protection with the Death of Domesticated Animals

People today know that the disease was spread at least in part by rodents and the fleas they carried. What is often overlooked, however, is that the Black Death did not just claim humans; it killed a fairly large percentage of the animals as well. This was a very serious problem since many of the livestock began to die off just as quickly as the people who managed them. At first, people were mostly concerned about contracting the disease, but they soon realized that they also needed to worry about their herds and animals.

Essentially all livestock were vulnerable to the plague, as well as animals like cats and dogs. The loss of cats and smaller dogs that killed the pests meant that the rodent population grew as the Black Death took the animals that preyed on them. This contributed to the further spread of the disease because there were fewer animals to stop the growing rodent population.

The other animals that began dying in alarming numbers included sheep, cows, goats, pigs, and chickens. All of these animals were major food sources. This meant that at a time when people were already combating the further spread of the illness, they were also facing the very real possibility of famine. As an increasing number of livestock animals died, there was no contingency plan for alternate food sources for the towns and cities that were far removed from the ocean and seas where fish was plentiful.

Wool Shortage

Sheep were also victims of the plague, and they died off in alarming numbers. Naturally, this was a concern in terms of food, but sheep supplied something else that people needed for survival—wool. This particularly versatile livestock died off in record numbers, leaving those humans who did not die of the disease to succumb to the cold of winter for lack of adequate warmth. Although it was not nearly as sensational as the loss of human life, the significant decline in the sheep population meant that the people would suffer for several years after the Black Death became less prevalent. There were not adequate numbers of sheep to supply the necessary wool for clothing, blankets, and other daily items. The wool shortage would affect the population long after they felt that they were safe from the plague itself.

Labor Shortage

The death of so many domesticated animals certainly was a blow to the people of Europe at this time. At the same time, there were not enough people to work with the animals or the land as was required to sustain the population living in the towns and cities. People had begun to move to the towns and cities, and there they died off in astonishing numbers. Although the rural areas were not as devastated as the cities and towns, those areas where the plague did visit typically lost nearly all of the laborers who worked the land or with the animals.

The result was a labor shortage that would affect all of Europe long after the fear of the plague had dissipated.

The members of the nobility and monarchs tried to lure people from the towns and cities back to the rural lands with very little success. Having already seen that there was little to gain from working the lands that belonged to other people, the general populace was not interested in returning to the fields. Laws were enacted to try to manage the problem. After all, there were practical reasons to have laborers—they were essential for growing the food that was sold in towns and cities. Higher wages were offered in the hopes of drawing people from the towns and cities to work the lands and other services. Beggars in the city streets were significantly reduced because anyone with the ability to work was needed. Essentially, the Black Death had created a market that better benefited the worker than the lords or nobility. This was not something that most countries had encountered before and provided the people with better means than they had prior to the outbreak. Only people who were disabled were allowed to receive any kind of alms or support.

Given that most people had previously found it difficult to find adequate pay for their work, this served as one of the few good things to come from the horrors of the 1340s to the early 1350s. It provided opportunities the general population likely would not have had otherwise. Even the Church began to hire people who were not qualified, as mentioned earlier. The problem was that many of the laws said that people were required to accept any work they were offered, and some of the wealthy tried to take advantage of this by offering less in wages than the work was worth, knowing that people would have to accept it instead of taking alms based on the law. On the whole though, it provided something that many people would not have gained if the Black Death had not arrived—a chance to get an education or training in trades or jobs that were more profitable.

Wars Stopped

One of the most intriguing (and positive) results of the spread of the Black Death was that the people in power had something far more pressing to occupy their time than trying to expand their empires through traditional means. Of course, there were people who tried to expand their power or influence through other means, but wars all but stopped during this time. King Edward III ceased his attacks on France, creating a temporary reprieve just a few years into the Hundred Years' War.

The Black Death has the distinction of taking the greatest toll of human life up to that point in European history. No war or other event had ever claimed so many lives, certainly not as rapidly as the plague did as it entered and ravaged country after country.

Initially, countries ignored the plague because it was focused on the cities in Italy. As it rapidly began to extend beyond the borders into nearly every country on the continent, wars almost entirely ceased to be waged. The people who survived the plague were needed to work the lands, not to wage wars. It was one of the few times in medieval Europe that rulers allowed peace to dictate their actions. It was not the kind of peace that anyone would want because people were fighting an enemy that was clearly far more lethal and extreme than any ruler, but it was still a notable change from the constant wars that are still associated with the time period. People think of knights and grand battles as being a staple of existence, yet for this period, all attention was focused on an entirely different kind of survival.

A Stronger Future

Most of the aftermath of the Black Death was negative, but for those who survived, particularly those who had contracted the plague but did not die, they became much stronger for the experience. According to studies conducted in 2014, one fact that was not realized following the ravages of the plague or the centuries after it was that the people who survived were a much healthier and hardier group. As horrific as the disease was, it can serve as proof of survival of the fittest, as the population of Europe who was old or infirm did not survive. Of course, the disease killed many healthy people as well, but there were some who did not die. This helped to provide some immunity for future waves of the disease. As the death toll was reduced and far fewer victims contracted the Black Death, the lifespan for most of the remaining Europeans was actually longer than before the plague struck.

The study focused on the bones of people in London cemeteries. According to their analysis of the human remains, only about 10% of the population would survive to their 70th birthday before the plague. Following the ravages of the Black Death, that percentage began to go up, nearly doubling over the next century or two. Scientists speculate that the people who died because of the plague could have had genetic deficiencies that would have shortened their lifespans. The deficiencies could have ranged from immune systems that were not as strong as those who managed to survive the disease to heart conditions that made some people less capable of fighting off the disease. Genetics was entirely unknown in those days, so the illness would have seemed entirely random, but it could have acted as a way of removing many of those who would have had a shorter lifespan normally. The people who survived may have had much stronger genetic makeups that were then passed on to their children, all the way to modern-day Europe.

Chapter 12 – Lasting Effects on Europe's Future

Europe was forever changed by the arrival of the Black Death on its shores. Its people would never again look at disease and illness as isolated events, even those illnesses that occurred far away. There were plenty of warning signs prior to the arrival of the disease in Europe, but those warnings went unheeded.

With the loss of between a quarter and half of the European population, it was a devastating blow to a people that had been largely unaffected by disease up until that time (that we know about). Only China seemed to suffer more profoundly, with an estimated half of the population dying because of the plague. As the place where the plague originated, it is easier to understand such a devastating toll in China. For a place as far removed from China as Europe was, there was ample time to try to prevent or at least minimize the problem should it arrive on their shores.

It took the loss of so much life and belief in the system for the people of the continent to realize they were not immune to the problems that persisted in other nations and on other continents. Today, people panic at the threat of an outbreak no matter how far away a disease is when it is first diagnosed. For example, the panic in the early part of the 21st century because of Ebola was far worse. Although the threat was far overstated, this is in large part because so many countries had learned how to take the necessary precautions to prevent the spread of disease. Our knowledge today can be directly linked to the experiences and lessons that people learned following the tragedy wrought by the Black Death. Health measures like quarantines and laws have ensured that deadly diseases stand less of a chance of spreading on anything like the same scale today.

Those lessons were also learned over the perpetual return of the plague over the next few centuries in Europe. The people were better equipped, and few countries suffered to such an extent again (with the exception of England which was very slow to implement protections). From the ashes and misery left in the wake of the Black Death, Europeans began to piece their lives together over the next few centuries.

Repopulation and the Roles of Women

One of the greatest challenges after the first occurrence of the Black Death in Europe was to repopulate. Royal and noble women were already treated as babymakers up to this time. Those who did not die during childbirth were shunted aside for mistresses once they outlived their usefulness so that kings could continue to procreate. Now the women of all of the different levels of society had an additional role, as it was essential that more children be produced. At the same time, there was a labor shortage, so they also had to work. Still, they were not granted any additional rights or respect by the patriarchal society in which they lived.

Of course, there were some powerful women who were more than a match for their male counterparts. These women not only bore children, but they often lorded over the men in their families. History tends to be particularly cruel to these women, but they were no worse than many of their male counterparts who are typically depicted in a different light.

As cities and towns began to recover, families like the de' Medicis began ascending to a power that they likely would not have attained had the Black Death not reached European shores. By the 1430s, the de' Medicis had risen from being successful bankers and traders to being one of the most powerful families in Italy (and Europe). They were one of the leading families during the Renaissance, and often the women in the family were as much in control as the men, although they were not able to hold the same kinds of official offices (particularly in the Catholic Church).

The constant resurgence of the plague made it nearly impossible for the population to recover in the decades following the initial wave. It would take several centuries for the population to recover, with the Renaissance being the first time when the population seemed to have returned to the same numbers as had been in Europe when the Black Death first entered.

Biological Warfare

Perhaps even more terrifying than an illness that you don't understand is the idea that people tried to figure out how to weaponize the illness to use against their enemies. It is a profoundly baffling thought process, particularly as most people saw the value in stopping wars as the plague swept across Europe.

Yet this was the lesson that some people learned from the Black Death. Perhaps inspired by the written records of de' Mussi, people would later begin to look for ways to turn the tragedy into a weapon.

Today, biological warfare is one of the most terrifying prospects that humanity faces. The Black Death has already proved that once released, there is absolutely no way for any human to control the way that an illness will spread. This has not stopped countries from trying to weaponize some of the worst illnesses that the world has seen. Although smallpox was declared to have been eradicated, it remains a serious concern. Vaccination has made it possible to prevent any natural spread of the disease (though some small pockets of society are fighting back and are making it possible for the disease to return through children and adults who are not vaccinated). While the natural occurrence of the disease has been all but stopped, several countries have found ways to weaponize this incredibly infectious and deadly disease. It was one of the major plagues that wiped out large portions of the world for over hundreds of years until the introduction of the vaccination, and that was bad enough without it being intentionally used to kill people.

Countries saw the destruction wrought by the disease and decided that it could be just as devastating if they turned it into weapons. Clearly, certain pockets of humanity are not any less barbaric or indifferent to the pain and devastation they could cause. Apparently, they also do not bother to learn from history because we have already seen how impossible it was to stem the Black Death in the early days. By changing a disease as deadly as smallpox and releasing it into the world today, there is no way that the offending country would be able to limit the spread of the disease. With planes and other efficient means of transportation, the release of a weaponized version of any disease is likely to have just as devastating an effect on the world's population as the Black Death.

The Black Death should be remembered for what it was—the first example of the power of disease and how humanity has nothing with which to combat a new disease. Typically, it takes years of studying a disease to fully understand how it interacts with the human body and how best to fight it. Weaponized diseases are meant to be more difficult to stop and would probably be just as much a tragedy as the first wave of the Black Death, if not worse.

The Name the Black Death

The people who experienced the Black Death did not call it that. It is not known exactly where or when the name originated, but people today as often as not refer to the first major European pandemic as the Black Death.

Historians believe that the name was a description of what the plague did to the victims. With some of the most renowned people of the time providing very descriptive passages about exactly what the disease did (most notably Boccaccio), it is easy to see how the plague got such a chilling name. The fact that it continued to literally plague the nations of Europe, the Near East, and the Far East for centuries, the descriptions were not entirely necessary because there were constant reminders of just what the bacterium would do to its victims.

Still, the name the Black Death typically relates to the very early instances of the plague in Europe and is not really used to denote the recorded cases that happen every year. People of the time typically called what was happening "the Pestilence." Over time, the panic and fear that the disease inspired faded as people learned how to combat it. Despite this, that first encounter left a serious scar on both the people who lived through it and the collective consciousness. Even today, mentioning the Black Death conjures up images of one of the darkest periods in European history. Nearly all of Western civilization has a rough idea of when it happened and the terrible toll of it.

The Black Death in Literature and Media

One way that we still remember this terrifying time is in our media and stories. For centuries, Western civilization has revisited and relived the Black Death from a safe distance. There is a morbid curiosity about it that comes through in nearly every piece of media.

There are many sites dedicated to it online, and debates about nearly every aspect of the Black Death rage on today, almost 675 years after it first reached Europe. People debate over how the disease spread, argue over the likelihood that the Tartars launched bodies over the fortifications in Caffa, and discuss the aftermath of the pandemic. Scientists and researchers dig up bodies that once terrified the survivors in the hopes of providing a more accurate picture of the disease, the consequences, and the aftermath.

Perhaps the most notable way that the Black Death still affects the people of European descent is in the works of fiction. The images and stories from this time have been retold, reworked, and reimagined in every possible medium that we use today. We provide happier endings for a few fortunate characters or create an alternate world where the continent was not so devastated. From books to fanfiction to video games, there is no medium that does not provide some means of recounting this dark time.

Nursery Rhymes and Other Legacies of the Black Death

The works of art that were inspired by the Black Death have survived through the centuries, and some are still known today. The works of Boccaccio and Petrarch are still renowned as they provide both a historical perspective and a literary eloquence that is unrivaled by any of their peers later in the Renaissance.

However, there is no piece of literature that has permeated the English-speaking world like a simple nursery rhyme.

>Ring-a-round the rosies
>
>A pocket full of posies
>
>Ashes! Ashes!
>
>We all fall down.

Today, children sing it while holding hands, then gleefully fall to the ground as they sing the last line of the rhyme. It certainly seems innocent, but what the nursery rhyme actually tells is a short version of the life of a plague victim. The ring described in the first line were the buboes that formed indicating that the victim had been infected by the plague. At this point, the victim would be aware that he or she very likely only had a few days left to live.

The second line refers to the flowers that people carried in their pockets hoping to ward off the disease. Not understanding exactly what caused the plague, anything was tried in the hopes that it would offer protection. The use of flowers seems whimsical, but it actually was seen as a possible ward against infection.

The third line can refer to several different things. Places like the port town of Bordeaux attempted to rid themselves of the mounds of corpses by burning them. This proved to be a disastrous decision as they could not control the fire. Most places opted to use mass graves as it became clear that individual burials would be impossible as cities, towns, and villages were gripped by the disease. In this case, ashes probably is a biblical reference. The King James Bible, Genesis 3:19, reads: "In the sweat of thy face shalt thou eat bread, till thou return unto the ground; for out of it wast thou taken: for dust thou art, and unto dust shalt thou return." This particular line is a reminder that when faced with the Black Death, everyone is equal. No person was too powerful, too wealthy, too religious, or too wise to escape being claimed by the terrible disease.

The inevitability of death and the feeling that everyone would eventually be claimed is represented by the last line. The laughter and giggles that typically accompany this line are in stark contrast to what the words mean. But who would want to deprive children of such a catchy rhyme that can put smiles on their faces?

The Masquerade of the Red Death

Since the publication of Boccaccio's *Decameron*, many writers have taken a shot at writing something that could earn them a fraction of the fame and renown that he gained through his work. There is only one author who managed to make anything even remotely as memorable, and he lived roughly 500 years later.

Considered one of the modern masters of short stories, Edgar Allan Poe wrote stories that tended to be morbid. Given the story of his life, it is understandable that he was drawn to the darker side of existence. This is perhaps why he was able to take a topic as complicated and grim as the Black Death and create a work of fiction that is easily understood by readers more than 150 years after his death.

The name of the story reflects the source of inspiration, "The Masquerade of the Red Death." It is a fairly short story that begins in a manner somewhat similar to Boccaccio's famous work. Poe does not spend a long time detailing the disease, but one paragraph is all that he needs to make it nearly impossible to miss that the Red Death of the story is a direct reference to the Black Death:

> No pestilence had ever been so fatal, or so hideous. Blood was its Avatar and its seal – the madness and the horror of blood. There were sharp pains, and sudden dizziness, and then profuse bleeding at the pores, with dissolution. The scarlet stains upon the body and especially upon the face of the victim, were the pest ban which shut him out from the aid and from the sympathy of his fellow-men. And the whole seizure, progress, and termination of the disease, were incidents of half an hour.

Obviously, the plague did not kill people within a half hour, but Poe's poetic license highlights just how impossibly fast the disease worked. Most illnesses kill people slowly, such as cancer and tuberculosis. By comparison, it seemed like the plague killed in the blink of an eye.

The story then goes on to follow Prince Prospero who fled the city and the misery of the Red Death along with his friends. They sought to wait out the disease in a remote location where they thought they would be immune from the ravages of it. The story is decidedly by Poe, and it ends as anyone familiar with his typical style would expect—death.

The parallels between what happens in his short story is more of a modern retelling of the events from one of the darkest periods of European history. It brings the horrors and fear into a more modern setting, even though it definitely is set in the past (even for the time it was written, the setting was from an earlier time).

His story concludes with what most of Europe recognized as a result of the Black Death. There was no easy escape from the plague. No amount of wealth, privilege, or power could save a person. The story is not exactly a gentle reminder, but it does serve to help remind people that no one can escape, making it more of a work of fiction for the general population during another period of time when the world was facing dark times.

Even more important, people who read this 150-year-old story can still tell that it is referring to the events from nearly 675 years ago. It is a testament to just how much the Black Death affected the collective minds of Western civilization.

Conclusion

Several years before the plague reached the shores of Europe, there were rumors and warnings about how devastating the disease was. Before 1348, Europe had no collective memory of a disease that engulfed the entire continent. Up until that time, diseases tended to be limited to a few regions, and they were considered a problem that was to be handled by those in power in the affected regions.

The Black Death was the first instance of a pandemic throughout Europe since the fall of the Roman Empire. At first, it was seen as a problem for Italy, but both the rapid way that it killed those who contracted it and how impossibly fast it spread meant that it soon became a problem for the entire continent. As people attempted to flee from areas where the disease was prevalent, they ended up spreading the disease much further. There was no way to flee or escape the disease once it reached a city, and there was no known cure.

The Black Death completely changed the power dynamics on the continent. Wars ceased as nations struggled to find a way to minimize the problem. It was a grim fate that no one could fathom.

People turned to the religion that had dictated so much of their lives up to that point. However, the clergymen were just as lost as the people, and they could only offer the same kinds of solutions that they had for everything else. It was a punishment from their God, and only prayer and repentance would stop it. This was quickly proved to be wrong as the rich, powerful, and clergy died in the same numbers as those of the regular people.

Everything that the people had known was called into question, but there was no time to really ponder how to resolve things because survival became the only challenge they had time to face. Some turned toward their worst impulses, using the Jewish population as scapegoats. Others tried to find a solution that agreed with their faith. Few countries were spared from the disease, and no social class, race, age, or gender was spared from its ravages. The writings of two of the most famous authors of the Middle Ages shed light on the daily lives of the people who experienced the disease. Today, these works are still studied to understand the difficulties they faced.

There were many long-lasting consequences of the disease, from too few people to work to food shortages to the wool shortage. As the Black Death seemed to go away, the people were forced to both deal with the aftermath and try to rebuild their lives. The aftermath included some positive aspects, some of which were not realized until centuries later. The silver lining to such monstrous storm clouds was nearly impossible to see for the years immediately surrounding the events. It is only through the distance of time that we can more fully appreciate how it positively changed the rigid social structures and inspired people to think for themselves. It would take several more centuries for these lessons and changes to fully take hold, but the Renaissance is in part a result of the way thinking began to change on the continent.

No matter how much time passes though, this frightful time in European history has not disappeared from the social consciousness. It is still a topic that is fiercely debated and studied. The Black Death never stopped inspiring art of all kinds as people continue to try to understand just how calamitous it was on the unsuspecting people who endured it. When it was all over, most historians estimate that it claimed at least a third of the European population. Something that devastating was sure to leave an indelible mark on the memory of all of the descendants of the survivors. Our artwork today proves that it still lives on in our memories, shaping our lives almost 700 years later.

Here's another book by Captivating History that you might be interested in

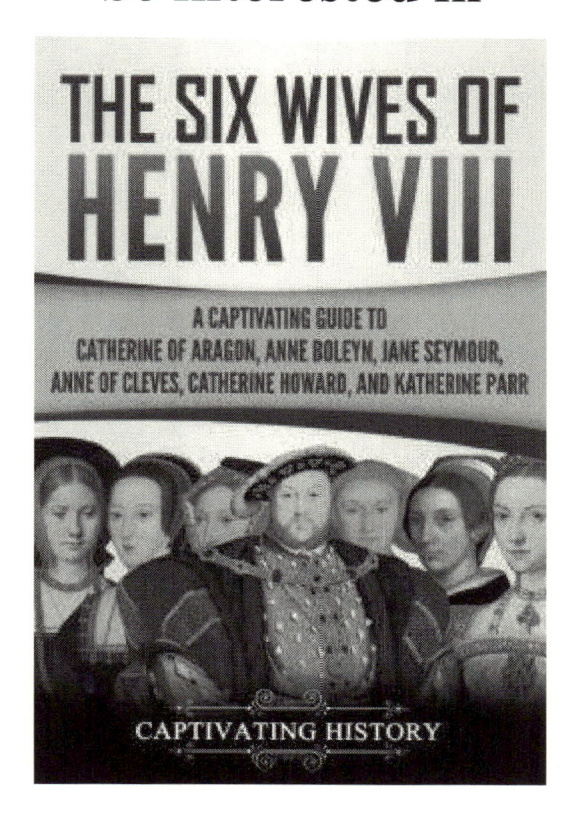

Free Bonus from Captivating History (Available for a Limited time)

Hi History Lovers!

Now you have a chance to join our exclusive history list so you can get your first history ebook for free as well as discounts and a potential to get more history books for free! Simply visit the link below to join.

Captivatinghistory.com/ebook

Also, make sure to follow us on Facebook, Twitter and Youtube by searching for Captivating History.

Bibliography

Biological Warfare at the 1346 Siege of Caffa, Wheelis, M. (2002), *Emerging Infectious Diseases*, *8*(9), 971-975.

Black Death Survivors and Their Descendants Went on to Live Longer. Pappas, S., May 8, 2014, Scientific American.

Black Death: Pandemic, Medieval Europe. *Encyclopedia Britannica*

Black Death. September 17, 2010, A&E Television.

Castilian Military Reform under the Reign of Alphonso XI, Clifford J. Rogers & Kelly DeVries.

Doctors of the Black Death, October 11, Jackie Rosenhek, Doctor's Review, Parkhurst.

Edward III, 2014, BBC.

Francesco Petrarca, September 2004, Yale University, Beinick Rare Book & Manuscript Library

In the Wake of The Plague: The Black Death & The World It Made, Norms F, Cantor, Simon & Schuster Paperbacks, New York 2001.

King James Bible, *Genesis 3:19*.

Labour after the Black Death. Lis, C. and H. Soly, "Labour Laws in Western Europe, 13th-16th Centuries," *Working on Labor*; 2012, pp. 299-321.

Lessons from the History of Quarantine, from Plague to Influenza A, Tognotti, E. (2013). Lessons from the History of Quarantine, from Plague to Influenza A. *Emerging Infectious Diseases*, *19*(2), 254-259. https://dx.doi.org/10.3201/eid1902.120312.

Masquerade of the Black Death, 25, 2017, Toni Mount, August, History Answers, Future Publishing Inc.

"The Masquerade of the Red Death," Poe, E. A, 1842.

Petrarch on the Plague, February 18, 2010, Decameron Web.

Plague in the United States, November 17, 2018, U.S. Department of Health & Human Services.

Plague, October 31, 2017, World Health Organization.

Plague. 2015-2019 National Geographic, LLC.

Plague. November 17, 2018, U.S. Department of Health & Human Services.

The Black Death 1348, 2001, Eye Witness to History, Ibis Communications, Inc.

The Black Death, by Charles River Editors: The History and Legacy of the Middle Ages' Deadliest Plague, Charles River Editors, November 2, 2018 San Bernardino CA, USA.

The Black Death, December 11, 2008, Church Influence on Society.

The Black Death, Philip Ziegler, Harper Torchbooks Harper & Row Publishers, New York.

The Black Death: And early Public Health Measures, 1999 - 2005, Brought to Life Science Museum

The Black Death. Horrox R, ed., Manchester: Manchester University Press; 1994. p. 14–2.

The Catholic Church and the Black Death in the 14th Century, 2018, Ivy Panda, Essay Samples.

The History of Plague – Part 1. The Three Great Pandemics. John Firth, JMVH 2019.

The Medici Family. November 9, 2009, History.com.

The Poe Museum, poemuseum.org.

The Rise of Towns: The International History Project, 2001, history-world.org.

The Threat: Smallpox. Center for Disease Control and Prevention, December 19, 2016.

What is a Pandemic? World Health Organization, February 24, 2010.

What is The Plague? 2005-2018, WEDMLLC.

Made in the USA
Middletown, DE
01 September 2021